COPTIC ORTHODOX PATRIARCHATE

MANY YEARS

WITH PEOPLE'S QUESTIONS

PART III

SPIRITUAL AND GENERAL QUESTIONS

By

H. H. POPE SHENOUDA III

Title	: Many Years With the People's Questions-Part III.
Author	: H. H. Pope Shenouda III.
Translated By	: Mrs. Glynis Younan - London.
Revised By	: Mrs Wedad Abbas.
Illustrated By	: Sister Sawsan.
Edition	: The second edition.
Typesetting	: J.C. Center, Heliopolis.
Printing	: Dar El Tebaa El Kawmia, Cairo.
Legal Deposit No.:	9839/1991.
Revised	: COEPA - 1997

H.H. Pope Shenouda III
117th Pope and Patriarch of Alexandria
and the See of St Mark

INTRODUCTION

This series which I am bringing out for you, dear reader, under the title **So many years with the problems of people**, contains those questions which I have been able to select for you from among the thousands which I have been asked, since the setting up of the Episcopate of Religious Institutions and Church Teaching in 1962, until today.

Its first part deals with questions concerning the Holy Bible, such as verses which appear difficult to understand, or which some people misinterpret, or which require explanation and clarification. In that part I have answered some forty questions which are repeatedly asked by many people.

The second part is concerned with questions of theology and doctrine which preoccupy people's minds. I have as far as possible taken care to preserve a style that would be easy for all to understand, and in that part I have replied to some thirty-five questions which might be of interest to all.

This third part concerns all kinds of spiritual questions, along with questions which circulate in society which require answering, such as a question about drinking wine, and another about organ transplants, and a third about how to solve problems, which I have answered in some detail.

This part comprises some forty-four questions in the majority of which I have taken special care to give an answer that is to the point. There is a fourth part which is at present being printed, and which I hope will be published soon, God willing, possibly only a couple of weeks after this book has reached your hands! With the help of your prayers, I shall continue to publish what answers I can to those questions which I consider to be most common and most important.

May all be well for you and may the Lord be with you.

February 1990

Pope Shenouda III

[1]

THE ORIGIN OF BAD THOUGHTS

Question?

Is every bad thought which goes round in my mind to be considered a sin? Where do these bad thoughts come from, and how can I stop them from coming?.

Answer:

Not every bad thought which goes round in your mind is to be considered a sin, for there is a difference between being under attack by thoughts and falling into sin through thoughts:

Being under attack by thoughts is when a bad thought harasses you, but you do not give in to it, but rather try with all your heart and might to banish it, even though it might remain for some time. When such a thought persists against your own wishes, it is not considered a sin. On the contrary, your resisting it could be credited to you as righteousness.

But falling into sin through one's thoughts is when you give in to bad thoughts and begin to take pleasure in them wishing to keep them, and perhaps even create new forms of them...

Falling into sin through one's thoughts may begin from a sinful desire in your heart or something stored away in your inmost mind. Or it may begin with an attack by the enemy from without, which you resist at first, but then surrender to, so that you fall and then get more and more entangled.

Or you may become lost in a thought for some moments and pleased with it, but when you come to your senses and wake up you regret and resist it, and so it flees from you.

The more you resist the thought, the more power you gain over it, so that it flees from you, or does not dare to assail you. On the other hand, the more you surrender to it, the more power it gains over you, and the more it is emboldened to attack you.

The rudder to steer the fight is under your control not under the control of your thoughts. Thoughts can really give you quite a shock and cause you grave concern and, depending on your situation, they may even wage war against you. The Lord Jesus Christ said, however, *"the ruler of this world is coming, and he has nothing in Me." (John 14:30)*. But what about **you**? When Satan attacks you, will he find he has a hold on you?!

The thought will search your heart first of all, to see whether there is anything in it which is akin to itself, since 'like attracts like', or whether it can find a point of correspondence to latch on to.

If your heart is very honest from within, it will not betray its master with these thoughts, nor let them gain entrance. It will have nothing to do with them, nor accept them, so that the thoughts end up fleeing away from your mind and the devils become afraid of it...

However if the heart is not careful about such thoughts and is lenient with them then they get the courage to assail that heart.

There are bad thoughts which enter a clean heart because of its lax or too easy-going attitudes.

There are bad thoughts which come out of a bad heart owing to its lack of purity.

That is to say there are bad thoughts which come from outside and others which come from inside.

An example of bad thoughts which come from outside, is that of the serpent's attack on Eve. Eve had a pure heart, but because she wasn't firm enough with the serpent, the ideas entered her heart and turned into desire and then into action.

Referring to those wicked thoughts which come from inside, our Lord said: " *an evil man out of the evil treasure of his heart brings forth evil." (Luke 6:45)*.

The thoughts may come from the heart, from hidden desires, or they may come from the inner mind, from images, ideas and information stored within.

From this mass that has accumulated within, thoughts come at any provocation and for any reason. So take care that what accumulates in you is pure.

However, the ideas which come from the mind are less powerful.

They are less powerful than the thoughts which come from the heart, because those that come from the heart are mixed with emotion or desire, and are therefore more powerful.

Thus it is easy for a person to banish the ideas which come from the mind. If he seeks to retain them or is willing to accommodate them, and doesn't resist them, they may move to his heart and become influenced by its emotional reactions and thus grow more powerful...

For this reason, a person should guard his heart as well as his mind, and should keep a dividing line between his head and heart.

"Keep your heart with all diligence, For out of it spring the issues of life." (Prov. 4:23). If the war of thoughts comes upon you, and you have a pure heart and are fervent in the Spirit, then it will be a weak fight, and one from which you can escape. But if it comes upon you while you are in a spiritually lukewarm state, or if your love for the Lord has grown cold, " *because lawlessness will abound* " *(Matt. 24:12),* then the fight will be a violent one and difficult to escape from. So, " *pray that your flight may not be in winter or on the Sabbath... (Matt. 24:20).*

Guard your mind so that nothing which could disturb its purity may enter. And guard your senses too, because they are the gates that lead to thought...

Guard your looks, your hearing, your touching and the rest of your senses. As you may not be able to prevent your mind from thinking about and being influenced by what you see and what you hear, it is better to be on your guard.

If something unsuitable reaches your ears, comes to your eyes, or enters your thoughts, do not let it go deep within you, but let it pass straight through.

Things which simply pass straight through do not have a very powerful effect, but if they go deep, they will settle in the innermost mind and extend their roots to the heart and may reach the stage of causing upsets.

Being able to forget is one of God's blessings to mankind, by which passing thoughts and transitory sensory perceptions can be wiped away.

But the ideas which you allow to enter deeply into you, settle in your inmost mind, and get to the conscious and subconscious, thus becoming difficult to forget. They might then form a reason for a war of thoughts and give rise to ideas, suspicions and dreams and become the source of desires and upsets, and the starting point of long stories...

We may need, however, to return to the subject of thoughts again.

[2]

ENVY

Question?

Does Christianity believe in the existence of envy?

Answer:

Envy, as a feeling, exists. We know, for example, that Cain envied his brother Abel, that Joseph the Righteous was envied by his brothers, and that the Lord Jesus Christ was handed over to death by the Jewish priests owing to their envy of Him.

At the end of the prayer of thanksgiving we say:
"Preserve us from all envy and every trial and act of Satan".

Envy exists, but an 'envious eye' is not something we believe in!

Some people believe that there are individuals who are envious by nature, such that if they should cast their envious eye someone, some accident will befall that person, so they are fearful of envy and of those who might be envious; whom they believe have the power to do evil. Sometimes they conceal the blessings which God bestows so generously on them for fear of envy, and they make up stories of this kind of envy that amount to little more than superstitious nonsense.

This kind of envy, we don't believe in, and we regard it as a kind of intimidation and unhealthy suspicion.

Envy does not harm the person who is envied, but rather the person who envies.

It doesn't harm the one who is envied, otherwise all those who have ever excelled or held foremost positions would have been exposed to envy and suffered loss, and likewise all who have ever obtained notable rank or state awards of distinction would have become the targets of envy and have been smitten by disaster or misfortune.

What we see however, is the opposite, which is that the one who envies lives a wretched and unhappy life as a result of his envy and inner misery, as the poet said:

"Bear patiently the deceitfulness of the envious, for your endurance will kill it; just as fire surely consumes itself if it finds nothing to feed on."

Why do we pray, then, to be preserved from envy, since it does no harm?

We do not pray out of fear of the so-called 'envious eye', but we pray that God will frustrate any harmful plots or deceitful tricks which the envious person might carry out against us because of their evil hearts.

When Joseph's brothers envied him, they threw him into a well, then sold him as a slave and were about to kill him. Cain killed his brother Abel out of envy and when the chief priests of the Jews were jealous of Christ, they conspired against Him and handed Him over to be crucified.

[3]

SHOULD ONE GIVE FROM TITHES TO RELATIVES?

Question?

Many people have asked me this question: If we have poor relations; a father, mother or sister etc., should we give to them out of our tithes?.

Answer:

Yes, of course one should give to the needy relatives from one's tithes. St. Paul the Apostle said " *if anyone does not provide for his own, and especially for those of his household, he has denied the faith and is worse than an unbeliever." (1 Tim. 5:8).*

However, it is not right to give **all** the tithes to relatives and neglect the other poor people who are not related to you, and that is for two reasons:

1. Lest what you give for your relatives should be a social duty which you are obliged to perform whether you pay tithes or not, or you pay it more on account of ties of blood than out of' compassion or sympathy for those in need, or with the purpose of carrying out the commandment.

2. Sometimes there may be poor people who are more in need than your relatives, and it would not be right for you to neglect them.

If you have needy relatives they can be given some of your tithes.

[4]

MY OWN FINANCIAL NEEDS AND PAYING THE TITHES

Question?

I wasn't able to pay any tithes at all last year, because of the pressure of economic burdens on me and my financial needs. What should I do? Can I be excused from paying the tithes?

Answer:

You are supposed to pay tithes irrespective of your financial situation. Here I would like to put before you some important observations which are:

1. Whoever pays his tithes when he himself is in need, will have a greater reward from God. Because by doing so he is putting others before himself, unlike the person who pays but is comfortably off and can well afford it, who does not feel that he is forgoing any of his necessities in order to supply the needs of another.

We observe that the Lord Jesus Christ praised the poor widow who paid the two small copper coins, and said that she had put more than all the others into the temple treasury because: *"for all these out of their abundance have put in offerings for God, but she out of her poverty put in all the livelihood that she had."(Luke 21:4) "she.... put in all that she had " (Mark 12:44).*

You too should become accustomed to giving, even though you are in need, whether you give of your money, time or health. The second remark I would like to make is:

2. When you give, even though you are in need yourself, God blesses whatever you have.

How often the needy person says: 'If all my money and all my salary aren't enough for me, whatever would happen if I also paid a tithe, a tenth of my income?! would the nine tenths be enough for me?!' But at this point I would like to say to you:

The nine-tenths with a blessing, is more than the whole lot without blessing!

Whenever you give, God blesses the little which remains, and makes it much more than all the money without the blessing of the tithes. He compensates you with more; and what else? The effectiveness of that money will be blessed. This comes in contrast to the many people who have wealth in abundance and yet feel as if they do not have enough because their wealth has no blessing.

The third observation which I would like to make is that:

3. God does not need our tithes, but He trains us and blesses us through them.

He trains us to give, and to love others, and to renounce money. He also trains us to have faith: faith in God's blessing of the small portion...

God is able to cater for all the needs of the entire world, without our paying anything. He is the One who satisfies all, from out of His good gifts, but He wants us to share in the act of charity, so that we may partake of the blessing of this act.

4. I know your financial circumstances. But put God to the test.

The general rule is: "*You shall not tempt the Lord your God.* " *(Matt. 4:7),* But the tithes are the one exception, and about this our Sovereign Lord said: "*Bring all the tithes... Prove Me now in this, says the Lord of hosts ' If I will not open for you the windows of heaven And pour out for you such blessing That there will not be room enough to receive it (Mal. 3:10).*

Thus test and see how God will bless your property, and see how you will not go needy, but on the contrary God will provide you with more and more.

Do not, however, pay the tithes merely with the objective of getting more and more...

For this is not the right spiritual attitude for giving. Just pay them even if you are going through a time of increased need yourself. For when God sees the sincerity of your heart when it comes to giving, along with your love for others, then He will open the floodgates of heaven as He has promised.

Hence, pay them and say: 'Who am I, Lord, that You allow me to share in the needs of Your children! ' *"Everything comes from You... it comes from Your hand, and all of it belongs to You." (1 Chr. 29:14-19)* 'So bless what little is left, O Lord, and let us want for nothing.'

Another point I would like to raise is:

5. The tithes which you do not pay are considered to be your wrongful possession.

It is money which is wrongfully yours because you have wronged its rightful owners - the poor who deserve it. It is not **your** money for you to keep. It is the Lord's property, and you have stolen from Him, thus God considers it as unlawful possession.

See what the Divine Inspiration says in the Book of the prophet Malachi: *"says the Lord of hosts... Will a man rob God? Yet you have robbed Me! But you say, 'In what way have we robbed You?' In tithes and offerings.".' (Mal. 3:7-8)*. Thus the Lord says:

"Make friends for yourselves by unrighteous mammon. (Luke 16:9).

What does this phrase mean then? it means:

6. With the money of the tithes which you have kept back for yourselves which has become an unlawful possession since you wronged the poor by not giving it to them... with this money

make friends for yourselves who will pray for you, and to whose prayers God will respond. Just as you saved them from their money problems when you paid the tithes, God will also rescue you from your financial problems...

A final word remains which I would like to say to you which is:

7. The tithes which you did not pay last year you still owe!

You are supposed to pay them, even if it is by instalment.

[5]

BEING NOSEY, AND PRYING INTO OTHER PEOPLE'S BUSINESS

Question?

I would like you to give me some advice on what to do about being nosey and over-curious about other people's affairs, because I suffer from this habit and want to be rid of it. I want to know how to stop being like this and how to avoid making this mistake.

Answer:

Being nosey, or prying, is a desire to know other people's secrets and personal affairs, whether it is through reading about them, or hearing or speaking about them, directly or indirectly.

Prying is something wrong, both from the spiritual and from the social point of view.

People are supposed to respect other people's secret and private affairs even within the family circle. For example, the father or mother does not have the right to open the son's letters. The husband or wife has no right to fish around in the pockets or drawers or papers of the spouse.

No one has a right to listen to words which are not meant for him to hear. We could call this 'infidelity of the ears'.' Nor is it anyone's right to look in secret at what he ought not to see. All this is a kind of spying on others which does not befit a spiritual person...

Prying or intruding into others' affairs, however, may be done openly, and not necessarily furtively.

An example of this would be a person who wears someone else out with questions about a matter that is personal to that other person, and about which he does not want to talk! Yet the nosey person goes on attacking him with questions, perhaps in great detail, in order to try and get everything out of him...

The nosey person may say, by way of excuse, that he has a close relationship with that other person, or that he wants to be reassured that that other person is all right.

But being in a close relationship with someone still has limits which one ought not to trespass against. Similarly the desire to be reassured about someone has its bounds. Finding out information does not come about through force or pressure. There is a vast difference between a person who wants to be reassured about someone, and a person who wants just to **know**, and to **know** everything!

Therefore, my advice to you is, not to ask, or if you notice a reluctance to answer in someone whom you have asked a question, or if you find him unwilling to elaborate further or go into all details of a particular matter, do not press him with any more questions.

One of the characteristics of the nosey or prying person is his insistence.

His friends and acquaintances often try to avoid him and avoid his many questions and his curiosity to know their business. This might annoy him, and he might complain about it, and they get embarrassed about revealing to him his nosiness, and their reluctance to answer his questions.

The most embarrassing of situations is when the nosey person meets a shy one.

The shy and timid person is not able to stop him and may be unable to change the course of the conversation to avoid the intrusive questions. Thus he is cornered and becomes embarrassed. The nosey person sees this embarrassment but does not care, because he wants to know, and what is more, he even wants to know the reasons for this embarrassment!

The prying individual may not be content with just knowing the inmost affairs of the person who is before him, but may even force him to reveal the secrets of someone else!

Not only does he ask that person about his affairs, but he also asks him about other people's. What that person said to them, and what they replied, what they did, what they felt in such and such a situation, how they behaved, and what their opinions were, what their relationship with the other person was, and about their families, their friends and private affairs ... !?

In fact, this may also lead to confessions in an embarrassing manner...

The senses of the nosey person always appear to be restless...

His gaze is never steady, but always brazen, never trustworthy, and he is noticeably on the alert. The same goes for his hearing, and his feet. He is never still, but always shifting about, going here and there, as he asks questions or listens, or worms his way into conversations which he has no claim to, and all in a most unseemly manner.

He may intrude in relationships which he has no right to know about, such as extremely private family relationships, such as those between husband and wife or between friends, be they men or women, or it may be secrets connected with work which ought not to be revealed. He may personally gain nothing whatsoever from all this, and he may well be unable to keep secret that which he has found out...

As far as you are concerned, when it comes to prying, my advice to you is:

1. Get into the habit of respecting other people's personal affairs, and be content that all individuals have the right to have their own private secrets which they do not have to tell even to

their dearest friends, just as you yourself have your own secrets.

2. Always ask yourself: what business is this of mine? Do I have any right to interfere in it? Say this to yourself, and you will be spared the embarrassment of someone else pointing it out to you.

3. Set limits to how close you get in your relationships with others.

4. If, on asking someone about a matter that is personal to him or to someone else, you should find him unwilling to answer, or if you sense an evasion or attempt to drop the subject, then don't press him further.

5. Do not try to read another person's letters, or rummage through his books or papers, and if any of them should happen to fall into your hands, then show proper respect by not trying to have a look at something which is none of your business.

6. Be honest and upright in all that you see, hear or touch.

7. Take care about your friends and acquaintances, so that. you do not lose them through prying into their personal affairs.

[6]

IS THIS VOW PERMISSIBLE OR FORBIDDEN

Question?

I vowed that I would keep on fasting until the war ended, and that was years ago. Is this vow legitimate or not?

Also, what is your opinion about someone who, for example, vows to have his child baptised in Jerusalem, or in one of the ancient monasteries in Upper Egypt? And again, what is your view on a young man who makes a vow of celibacy?.

Answer:

The Bible in fact says: *"Better not to vow than to vow and not pay. " (Eccl. 5:5).*

A vow is an expression of an agreement between a human being and God, so there is no going back on it.

The vow, however, must be healthy from the spiritual point of view, though, because it is not good to form an agreement with God in which there is something at fault.

On one occasion the Jews vowed to remain fasting until they had killed the apostle Paul *(Acts 23:12)*. Their vow was wrong and unlawful...

So not every vow is according to God's will, some vows might not be lawful.

Jephthah the Gileadite vowed that if he was victorious, he would sacrifice as a burnt offering whatever thing first came out from the door of his house to meet him on his return. *(Judg. 11:30)* And even though he was met by his young daughter, he fulfilled his vow and sacrificed her as a burnt offering to the Lord! To be sure, God would not have approved of this action at all, for the vow was for something not permissible. The Lord never commanded in His holy law that human beings should be offered as burnt sacrifices!

Concerning the parents vowing to have their child baptised at some far off place, they might actually be endangering the fate of their child. Suppose circumstances should, for example, prevent their reaching that place, or if the child should die before being baptised, how could they carry the responsibility of his eternal life? Also, the child's being deprived of partaking of the holy sacraments, until such time as circumstances made it possible for him to be baptised (according to his parents' wishes), would mean that he was being deprived of heavenly grace and blessings which could otherwise be at work within him. And the parents in this case would bear the responsibility for this before God.

So this kind of vow is completely wrong, especially since the effect of baptism does not change from one place to another, but is the same.

Receiving the blessing of a particular place, however, or of a particular saint, considering the risk involved, must be a matter confined to being purely one's personal wish. It should not ever be elevated to the level of becoming a vow.

It is the risk involved which makes us judge this case from the theological point of view by taking into consideration the possibility of this vow being broken, for our lives are in the hands of God, and a child can die even though he is perfectly healthy.

If the child's health was in danger, then the vow would have to be broken, thus the sin of breaking a vow would be committed, which is less serious than the death of a child unbaptised, and by breaking the vow, we would have chosen the lesser of two evils.

In both cases, the Church's disapproval is incurred by those who made the vow, i.e. the parents.

Generally speaking, these things should be made a matter of personal wishes rather than vows. People should pray about them and say: '0 Lord, we would very much like to have our child baptised in the holy place of such and such'. But they shouldn't vow. And at the same time, even if it is only a personal wish, they should not be slow in carrying it out, for the Bible says: " *When you make a vow to God, do not delay to pay it.* " *(Eccl. 5:4)..*

When it comes to the vow of celibacy, or the vow of monasticism, I do not advise these to be made by young people, or by those who have only recently become acquainted with the spiritual life...

It is not forbidden, because there is nothing wrong with it in itself, but there is a risk that the idea might be just the result of a temporary enthusiasm, or a passing influence. Or if the one who has made such a vow should suddenly be afflicted by severe spiritual attacks from the point of view of his body, he may regret having made the vow, and want to go back on it, or yearn to get married, or end up living in sin.

Instead of making a vow of celibacy, present your wish as a desire, and make it a matter of prayer to God.

Say to Him: 'I should **like**, O Lord, to be celibate, or become a monk. Please grant me this desire, **If it is according to Your will.**

As for those who are grown up and spiritually mature, who have tested themselves for a long time, and whom heavenly grace has helped along the path to victory, then there is nothing to prevent them from consecrating themselves to God. Even so, I would advise them not to delay too much in case the opponent stirs up uncalled for attacks against them.

As far as the vow of fasting until the end of war is concerned, this is not something practical.

Whoever said that wars on earth would come to an end?! They are ever present and, according to the Bible, will remain so until the end of the world. *(Matt. 24)* If, however, the vow concerns a specific war in a definite place, and if the one making the vow is mature, and capable of fasting, then there is no objection in this case.

When it comes to fasting, though, and the vows of celibacy and monasticism, it is necessary to ask advice from one's spiritual father.

It would not be right for a person to pursue these matters according to his own ideas, without having received guidance. If he were not to ask advice from his spiritual father in such important cases as these, then what would he ask him about?!

As a general rule, a person making a vow should not pronounce it quickly.

It requires reflection, thought, advice and prayer, however, before making the vow...

[7]

THE FIRST SIN

Question?

What was the first sin which the world came to know ?

Answer:

The first sin which the world recognised was that of pride...

It was the first sin into which Satan fell when he said: "*I will exalt my throne above the stars of God... I will be like the Most High.* " *(Is. 14:13-14).*

This was the first sin which mankind was attacked by, when the devil said to Eve: "*you will be like God, knowing good and evil.* " *(Gen. 3:5).*

When the Lord was incarnated, He fought this sin through His humility, by taking the form of a slave and becoming like a human being in His appearance, and by being born in a stable, and permitting the d`evil to test Him.

[8]

RESPONSIBILITY FOR A SIN WHICH ONE HAS NOT COMMITTED

Question?

If circumstances hinder me from my actually committing a sin (which I had been intending to commit), can it still be counted against me as a sin, even though I have not done it?.

Answer:

You might imagine, my friend, that the only form of sin is the sinful act! In fact the action is only the final stage of the sin, for sin begins first in the heart, with the love of evil and the heart's responding to it, then it enters into the stage of being carried out. If it is carried out, then it will have reached completion. But if it is not carried through, then the person can still be found guilty for the sin in his heart, for his desire, his intention and his thoughts.

What was Satan's sin if it wasn't the sin of the heart, when the Divine Inspiration said to him: "You said in your heart, 'I will ascend to heaven; I will exalt my throne above the stars of God... I will be like the Most High." *(Is. 14:13-14)*. Merely saying that in his heart was enough to make him fall from the height of his rank

[9]

IS SOCIAL SERVICE THE WORK OF THE CHURCH OR THAT OF THE STATE?

Question?

If the Church become involved in the sphere of social service, would it not have entered the area of the State's activity, and thereby 'lose its spiritual action' (as I read that one of the Fathers once described it)? would it not have gone beyond the realm with which Jesus Christ was concerned, seeing that He said: "My kingdom is not of this world"? would it not also be contradicting the teaching of the gospel?

Answer:

The Lord Jesus Christ was active in both these areas alike.

He was concerned with the spirit and with the body as well. The Bible says: " *Jesus went about all Galilee, teaching in their synagogues, preaching the gospel of the kingdom, and healing all kinds of sickness and all kinds of disease among the people.(Matt. 4:23).*

He preached on the mount in the desert, in people's homes, and on the shore of the lake: this is the missionary activity. The Bible also says: " *When the sun was setting, all those who had any that were sick with various diseases brought them to Him; and He laid His hands on every one of them and healed them. demons also came out of many, crying out..." (Luke 4:40-41).*

Thus healing the sick was not something beyond the bounds of Christ's work, and did not conflict with His saying: "My kingdom is not of this world".

If the Church then shows concern for healing the sick and founding hospitals and health services, it will not have gone beyond its spiritual mission, for the Church's mission is not only preaching, as we call it, but also to alleviate people's pains.

Our Lord gave us the parable of the Good Samaritan who, on finding someone who had been attacked, at the side of the road, bandaged that person's wounds and took him away on his donkey until he came to an inn where, at his own expense, he had the victim put up until he recovered. *(Luke 10:30-37).*

In this parable, the Lord directed His rebuke towards the priest and the Levite, who both showed no concern for the injured man and his plight. Jesus considered the action of the Good Samaritan to have been one of love and compassion.

Should the Church hold itself back from acts of love and compassion and give as an excuse that these are really the work of the State? No, not at all. Acts of kindness are required from every human being. The State is to do them and the Church too, and also each individual.

We should not consider these things to be just social service, but rather look on them as acts of love which are, after all, among the first fruits of the Holy Spirit *(Gal. 5:22),* and upon which depend the whole law and the Prophets, according to Christ *(Matt. 22:40).*

The Lord Jesus Christ was just as interested in feeding people as He was in preaching.

The miracle of the five loaves and the two fishes is mentioned in all four gospels. How beautiful were the words of Christ to His disciples when He said to them: *"You give them something to eat. " (Luke 9:13).*

In this commandment, then, was an order to the Church to feed the hungry. Although Jesus Christ was preaching to the crowds that day, He was not content just to preach, as if He regarded that alone as His kingdom, or His only concern.

When His disciples asked Him to send the crowds away to the neighbouring villages, so that they could buy food for themselves, the Lord answered them firmly, saying that He would not send them away hungry, lest they *"... faint on the way. " (Mark 8:3).*

It is a lesson to the Church not to be content just with preaching and words, but to feed the hungry too, not to imagine that in doing so we go beyond the mission of the kingdom, or to go outside the sphere of the religion or spiritual activity.

See what the apostle James says; " *Pure and undefiled religion before God and the Father is this: to visit orphans and widows in their trouble, and to keep oneself unspotted from the world." (James 1:27)*

If the church establishes orphanages, and concerns itself with helping the widows and the poor in their distress, will it be deviating from its original mission?! Would this not rather be the "religion" that God our Father accepts as pure and faultless?! This is the teaching of the Bible, not the teaching of man.

Trying to keep oneself unpolluted by the world is not enough, if one shuts oneself off inside from caring about the poor or the orphan. A priestly father cannot see a needy family and neglect to care for it, by making an excuse that it is the responsibility of the State to care for it! The State itself does not say so...

See how St. James the Apostle rebukes us saying: " *If a brother or sister is naked and destitute of daily food, and one of you says to them, "Depart in peace, be warmed and filled," but you do not give them the things which are needed for the body, what does it profit?" (James 2:15-16).*

Thus we see how the Church has concerned itself with these things right from the apostolic age, just as when the seven deacons were being consecrated because they found that some of the " *their widows were neglected in the daily distribution.* " *(Acts 6:1).*

In order that the apostles could devote themselves to the ministry of the Word, they appointed seven deacons, laying their hands upon them, so that they could undertake this service. Rather than say that the Church's work was not concerned with the administering of the provisions, they actually created a group within the Church to perform this function. No one ever ventured to say that this work was not God's work, but Caesar's!

The Book of Acts not only says that: "*With great power the apostles continued to testify to the resurrection of the Lord Jesus...* ". but also mentions directly afterwards that; " *Nor was there anyone among them who lacked; for all who were possessors of lands or houses sold them, and brought the proceeds of the things that were sold, and laid them at the apostles' feet; and they distributed to each as anyone had need.*" *(Acts 4:33-35)*. This teaching is the sound and pure gospel word.

The Church cannot hold back from helping the poor and orphans, widows, the sick and the hungry, as if out of some kind of deference to the State, as if it were afraid of offending it by encroaching on its preserves. This would not be to show courtesy to the State, but rather a lack of cooperation with it.

It would also show a failure to obey the commandments of the gospel, and would be a departure from the commandment of love, which the Bible states is the greatest of virtues *(1 Cor. 13)*. To do this would clearly be to fight against the Church and its mission, and would be an attempt to create a wedge between itself and the State at the present time, for the Church is the most loyal institution in the State and the State encourages the charitable works which the Church undertakes.

Let us record here that the Lord Jesus made these actions of love, which could also be referred to as social work, one of the bases of judgement on the Last Day.

He will say to those who stand on His left on the Day of Judgement: *"Depart from Me, you cursed, into the everlasting fire prepared for the devil and his angels: 'for I was hungry and you gave Me no food; I was thirsty and you gave Me no drink; 'I was a stranger and you did not take Me in, naked and you did not clothe Me, sick and in prison and you did not visit Me.' (Matt. 25:41-43)*.

Will they say to Him: 'We are sorry, but that was Caesar's business, not the work of God, and You told us to give to Caesar what was his and to God what was God's'?! or will they say to Him: 'Why are you so concerned about them, Lord, since Your kingdom is not of this world'?! Will they actually go to the fire prepared for them, for having neglected the work of love which society nowadays calls 'social service'?!

If this service is the duty of every person, how much more, then, should the Church give a good example! For the Church, after all, consists of Christ's disciples following in the footsteps of their Master and Teacher who first showed the way.

This service which we give to the poor, we are really giving to Christ himself, for He said: *"Assuredly, I say to you, inasmuch as you did it to one of the least of these My brethren, you did it to Me. " (Matt. 25:40).*

In Paul's letter to the Romans, he speaks about the Church's ministry to the poor, and the cooperation of the churches of Macedonia, Achaia and Jerusalem in this regard, and he said: " *But now I am going to Jerusalem to minister to the saints. For it pleased those from Macedonia and Achaia to make a certain contribution for the poor among the saints who are in Jerusalem. It pleased them indeed, and they are their debtors. For if the Gentiles have been partakers of their spiritual things, their duty is also to minister to them in material things." (Rom. 15:25-27).*

And he also said: " *distributing to the needs of the saints, given to hospitality. " (Rom. 12:13)*

Serving the poor and needy is not only social work, besides being an act of love, but is also a way of protecting the poor person from doing wrong.

It is this spiritual aspect of this service which is the essence of the Church's activity.

Poverty may drive the poor person to steal, to lie or to cheat, or to complain and blaspheme against God and against the Church, and thereby let his faith weaken. But when the Church gives to the poor person, it is making him aware of God's love for him, and making him feel that God has sent someone to provide for him, a matter which strengthens his faith.

For this reason, the social work which the Church undertakes has a spiritual character which distinguishes it. The spirituality of the commandment enters into it and is mingled with the word of teaching.

The majority of churches refer to the poor as the 'brothers of Christ' because that is what Christ called them *(Matt. 25:40)*, and they treat them as such when it comes to giving to them.

The Church finds a blessing in this service and carries it out in a spirit of a mother church with a father priest looking after their children.

The Church has engaged in these services and organised them since earliest times, and still does so today, and will continue to do so, if God wills.

Only the communist countries have limited the Church in its service, which they have done by confining it to performing the role of prayer only, whilst retaining everything in the hands of the State, because the state does not want there to be any link between the believers and God.

Communist thinking does not agree with the needy person receiving from God's house, for if he does so he will remember God and the men of God, and will retain his faith.

They do not want a believer to thank God for His grace and His offerings to him. They want any thanks to be given to the state alone, thus God disappears and does not compete with the state.

We meant here to warn against such thoughts lest they should be included unintentionally in any writings or cited or admired by any person not being aware of their danger.

We thank God that we are in a country where God is seen as being the origin of every blessing and every gift. We therefore encourage the people to have a close relationship with God.

The Church never participates in the work of the State, and never gets involved in politics, for politics is the State's activity.

Pastoral work, however, has a character all of its own, and the Church undertakes its pastoral work and concerns itself with its children. It does not think of religion as merely beliefs and ideas, or just sermons and preaching, for religion is above all, love. Love is that we show concern for providing our children with whatever good things we can.

[10]

HYMNS SUNG TO POPULAR TUNES

Question?

What do you think of hymns being set to popular tunes?.

Answer:

Those who set the words of hymns to popular tunes are only concerning themselves with the abstract idea of setting words to music, while ignoring the effect of the music on the soul.

Music can plant certain feelings in the soul. A piece of instrumental music, i.e. one without words, is able to make a person feel happy or sad. It can stimulate or excite him, or arouse some desire in him. We ought not to forget the powerful effect that music can have on the soul.

A hymn is a spiritual song and its music should be spiritual and its melody sacred.

It is not right for us to mix it with some other tune which might arouse different feelings apart from the holy and spiritual ones which the hymn is intended to arouse.

It is also likely that the singer will be reminded of the popular song and its words, and his mind or heart will wander or get mixed up with his emotions. We must remember, brothers and sisters, the words of the apostle: " *For what fellowship has righteousness with lawlessness?* " *(2 Cor. 6:14).*

[11]

HOW TO RESIST THOUGHTS

Question?

How can I resist thoughts which from time to time weigh heavily upon me and which try to force me to surrender to them?

Answer:

Occupy your leisure with some other stronger thought to take the place of such thoughts...

Do not wait until such thoughts have completely worn you out, before trying to resist them, for it is better - if you are able - not to give them any opportunity at all to reach you in the first place. But how does one do that?

Always occupy your mind with what is useful, so that if the devil wants to mount an attack upon your thoughts, he will find your mind occupied and not taking any notice of his ideas, so he will pass you by. Thought becomes extremely difficult once Satan has come to a person and found his mind wide open and ready to accept his ideas!

If a nasty thought comes to you, replace it with some other idea, for your mind cannot think of two subjects at the same time to the same depth. It is therefore necessary that the new thought, with which you want to cancel out the attacking thought, must be deep enough to banish the other. It could be, for example, thinking of a tricky problem, a difficulty, or question of faith, or some topic that interests you, or remembering something you have forgotten.

Superficial thinking will not banish the thoughts that are attacking you. The only thing that can do this is thinking other types of thoughts which can enter deeply into your mind or heart, such as thinking about an important family problem or some abstruse question that is difficult to solve, or about a subject that is dear to your heart which you enjoy dwelling on.

Another solution is to banish the thought by reading.

But again it has to be reading of a sufficiently deep nature to occupy the mind fully, because light reading provides the scope for the mind to wander, so it roams freely and is still distracted by what is attacking it.

Therefore, suppose a person is attacked by the thought of lust. Ordinary spiritual reading would not be as useful for him as would, for example, reading about solving problems in the Bible, or about doctrinal differences or refutations of them, or about some new subject which he hasn't studied before, or a scientific problem which requires concentration.

Unwanted thoughts can also be banished by prayers and prostrations.

For while the individual feels ashamed of, or embarrassed about thinking his wrongful thoughts when addressing God, he at the same time draws help from the prayer, provided, of course, that his prayer is made with fervour and feeling, and resists any tendency to wander from the point. Prayer accompanied by prostrations is even more powerful...

Attacking thoughts can also be driven away by engaging oneself in manual work.

It is because this activity likewise occupies one's thoughts and diverts them from being under attack, just as much as an activity that requires attention and concentration.

Work also occupies a person and relieves him of the war being waged against his thoughts, in contrast to having nothing to do, which gives scope for an attack on his mind. This is why the Fathers said that if a person works, only one devil attacks him, but if he does not, then he will be attacked by several. Notice how God gave our forefather Adam work to do while he was in the Garden of Eden, even though he did not need to work to provide for himself.

If the offending thought is not banished by all this, then the best thing is for the person to break out of his isolation and speak to someone else.

For it will be difficult for him to talk on one subject while his thought are on another. In fact any kind of amusement, whether it is pursued alone or in the company of others, can also help to drive away relentless thoughts.

The important thing is that you don't let yourself remain alone with those thoughts, or allow them to be your only concern.

Deflecting one's thoughts, or replacing them, or diverting the mind from them by some kind of activity or entertainment, conversation, reading, writing or prayer, can all weaken the attack upon one's thoughts, banish it, or make you forget it.

You also have to recognise the cause of the thought and deal with it.

For instance, a thought of anger or revenge may occur to you on account of a certain subject inside you, which needs to be dealt with and dispensed with. This is because as long as the reasons for anger remain within you, then thoughts of it will continue to attack you, however much you try to banish them.

If the thoughts have come from reading something in particular, or from listening to other people, or from some stumbling of the senses, or from a problem that is bothering you, try to protect yourself against all this, or find a solution for it, and thereby stem the original cause of the ideas.

If the thought of pride or false glory overcomes you, and there is a reason for that, you must fight this pride in your heart in a spiritual way. If you triumph over it, then those thoughts will leave you...

This is the method for you to follow in order to deal spiritually with thoughts of any kind of sin that you are attacked by.

In all of this you need to act quickly, and not be soft on yourself when it comes to such thoughts.

If you drive away the thought quickly, it will grow weak before you. But if you give it a chance, it will grow strong and you will grow weak trying to resist it. Then it may even combine itself with other ideas and branch out further, just as it may also move from the mind to the heart, and turn itself into desire or craving.

Be on guard against the way that excessive curiosity can deceive and mislead you.

A person may hang on to an idea or thought, with the excuse that he wants to know what it will result in, and in which direction it is leading, out of a kind of inquisitiveness!! You yourself actually know very well the likely outcome of a good many ideas, and if you don't, then you can at least deduce it from the way they have begun! So what use is it to be so curious, if it is only going to lead you astray?

There is another way, which is to counter the thought:

St. Evagrius laid down a method of renouncing thoughts with verses from the Bible. For every sin that attacks a person, there is a verse which can be put before it to reject it and calm it down. in the temptation on the Mount, the Lord rejected Satan's taunts with verses from the Scriptures.

There are thoughts, however, which require a swift repulsion, without any debate or discussion.

For to discuss them may invite such thoughts to become more permanent, and prolong their stay, besides causing them to branch out.

Thus if thoughts, which you ought to block quickly, should come to you, do not be sluggish or delay in doing so, nor wait to see where they might lead, and don't negotiate with them or have anything to do with them. For the more you hold on to such thoughts, the stronger they will get, and the more they will overpower you, whereas when they first come, they are still weak and you can more easily banish them.

Banishing thoughts calls for wisdom, discernment and assistance.

Some people are experienced at identifying and combating unwanted thoughts and, as St. Paul noted, we are not ignorant of the wiles of Satan. If anyone doesn't have experience in this, he should ask a spiritual guide. Generally speaking, divine assistance that comes with prayer and humbling oneself, helps to eliminate such thoughts.

The Lord is able to banish Satan and all his wicked thoughts.

[12]

LOVING ONE'S ENEMIES

Question?

What did the Lord mean in the gospel by His words: "*Love your enemies?.* " *(Matt. 5:44).* How can that be done?.

Answer:

Loving one's friend is something ordinary and found even among pagans and unbelievers. Loving one's enemy however is the highest and noblest moral virtue which the Lord desires of us. He wants us to hate evil, but not those who do it. We are to hate the sin, but not the sinner. Sinners are only the victims of misunderstanding, or of the Devil. We must love them and pray for them, so that they will stop acting like that.

How we are to do that is by following these points:

1. Not bearing hatred in our hearts towards anyone, however much wrong he has done us. For no hatred can dwell in the heart which houses love.

2. Not rejoicing at all, at any misfortune that should strike one who has done us harm, for the Bible itself tells us that: "*Love does not rejoice in iniquity...* " *(1 Cor. 13:6).* We should rather feel sorry that some harm has befallen our enemy.

3. We should counter evil with love and goodness, and by doing so, change the feelings of the one who wants to do us wrong. As St. John Chrysostom said: "There is a way of being rid of your enemy, and that is to turn him into a friend."

4. Confronting hostility with hostility only serves to inflame it, while keeping silent in the face of hostility, will simply cause it to stay as it is. But confronting hostility with love, heals it and makes it disappear.

5. Therefore, do not speak evil against your enemy, in case the hostility of him heart increases. But instead, do the opposite. If you find in his anything good, praise him for it, for this will help to change his feelings towards you.

6. If your enemy falls into difficulties, go to help him, for the Bible says: " *If your enemy is hungry, feed him; If he is thirsty, give him a drink;* " *(Rom. 12:20).*

7. The Bible also says: "*Do not be overcome by evil, but overcome evil with good.* " *(Rom. 12:21).* If you confront hostility with hostility, evil will have overcome you... Whereas if You confront it with love, then you will have overcome evil with good.

[13]

PUNISHMENT AND THE AGE OF GRACE

Question?

Some people say that there shouldn't be any punishment in Christianity, in view of the fact that we are now living in the age of grace, and that if punishment does exist, it will be in heaven, and not on earth. Is this true?.
Is punishment incompatible with God's love and grace, as it was shown on the cross?

Answer:

Divine grace cannot be in conflict with divine justice. God's grace is not at the expense of His justice, nor is it diminished by it!.

We should not just imagine God as being loving in the New Testament, and vengeful in the Old. God is the same yesterday, today and for ever... He was loving in the Old Testament, yet punished sin, and He is loving in the New Testament, where He also punishes.

David said about the God who punished in the Old Testament:

"He has not dealt with us according to our sins, Nor punished us according to our iniquities. For as the heavens are high

above the earth, So great is His mercy toward those who fear Him; As far as the east is from the west, So far has He removed our transgressions from us". (Ps. 103:10-12)

In the New Testament, the love of God was made manifest on the cross, totally blended with His justice, "abounding in love and faithfulness. " *(Ps. 86:5).*

God's justice and His punishing appear in the Bible, in many parables in the New Testament. and have appeared throughout history.

Probably one of the most striking examples of His punishment to men is the story of Ananias and Sapphira.

They received their punishment from God through the mouth of the apostle Peter. Ananias dropped down dead, because he had lied against the Holy Spirit, and when his wife, Sapphira, joined in that lie, Peter said to her: *" How is it that you have agreed together to test the Spirit of the Lord? Look, the feet of those who have buried your husband are at the door, and they will carry you out." Then immediately she fell down at his feet and breathed her last. And the young men came in and found her dead, and carrying her out, buried her by her husband. So great fear came upon all the church and upon all who heard these things. " (Acts 5:9-10).*

The punishment of Ananias and Sapphira took place on earth. It wasn't confined to the afterlife.

The same goes for the punishment of Elymas the Sorceror, for he opposed Saul and Barnabas, so that Saul was filled with the Holy Spirit and said to him: " *you enemy of all righteousness,... And now, indeed, the hand of the Lord is upon you, and you shall be blind, not seeing the sun for a time." And immediately a dark mist fell on him, and he went around seeking someone to lead him by the hand.. " (Acts 13:10-12)*.

One of the punishments which is famous in Christianity is that of ostracism.

St. Paul rebuked the people of Corinth for not punishing the sinner in their midst, saying to them: " *I have written to you not to keep company with anyone named a brother, who is sexually immoral, or covetous, or an idolater, or a reviler, or a drunkard, or an extortioner; not even to eat with such a person. " (1 Cor. 5:11)*. And he also said to them: " *put away from yourselves the evil person " (1 Cor. 5:13)*.

The apostle who spoke most about love, St. John, also spoke about this punishment of ostracism, saying: " *If anyone comes to you and does not bring this doctrine, do not receive him into your house nor greet him; for he who greets him shares in his evil deeds.." (2 John 1:10-11)*.

One of the hardest punishments of the New Testament was that of the sinner of Corinth. For St. Paul said: " *For I indeed, as absent in body but present in spirit, have already judged (as though I were present) him who has so done this deed. In the name of our Lord Jesus Christ, when you are gathered together, along with my spirit, with the power of our*

Lord Jesus Christ, deliver such a one to Satan for the destruction of the flesh, that his spirit may be saved in the day of the Lord Jesus.." (1 Cor. 5:3-5).

So, here is another instance of punishment taking place on earth.

One of the famous punishments also in Christianity was that with which God punished King Herod for being proud.

When the King approved of the people's saying to him: " *The voice of a god and not of a man!*" *Then immediately an angel of the Lord struck him, because he did not give glory to God. And he was eaten by worms and died.. (Acts 12:22-23)*.

There are many punishments described in the Book of Revelation, such as the punishments which will strike the earth when the seven angels sound their trumpets. John says that after the fourth angel's trumpet: " *And I looked, and I heard an angel flying through the midst of heaven, saying with a loud voice, "Woe, woe, woe to the inhabitants of the earth, because of the remaining blasts of the trumpet of the three angels who are about to sound!" (Rev. 8:13)*. And there are a lot more punishments described in this Book too!

The Lord Jesus Christ mentioned punishment at the beginning of his Sermon on the Mount,

He said: " *But I say to you that whoever is angry with his brother without a cause shall be in danger of the judgment. And whoever says to his brother, 'Raca!' shall be in danger of the council. " (Matt. 5:22)* So here is a form of punishment which was to be carried out on earth, which was different from the punishment of " *But whoever says, 'You fool!' shall be in danger of hell fire* " *(Matt. 5:22)*.

Then there is the punishment of excommunication, or eternal condemnation.

According to St. Paul: " *But even if we, or an angel from heaven, preach any other gospel to you than what we have preached to you, let him be accursed. As we have said before, so now I say again, if anyone preaches any other gospel to you than what you have received, let him be accursed." (Gal. 1:8-9)*

I should like to add, though, that punishment can be a sign of love. The Bible says: " *For whom the LORD loves He chastens. " (Heb. 12:6)*. Thus punishment is not incompatible with love, and does not contradict the work of heavenly grace, for punishment has often been the reason for souls to come to their senses, to wake up and safeguard their eternal life. This is real love, for if the sinner were to be left on earth without love, he would probably end up in a state of indifference and not caring, and thus perish, which would not accord with God's love for sinners.

The Church rules are full of punishments for sinners.

These rules have been laid down by the Spirit of God, through the Apostolic Fathers and the holy councils, and the great saintly Fathers. They include lots of penalties, and come within the framework of the belief of the Orthodox Christian.

But they do not differ from the spirit of the Bible, as I have said.

The lowest level of the well-known punishments is that of reprimand.

St. Paul said to his disciple Titus: " *exhort, and rebuke with all authority.* " *(Titus 2:15).* And in fact he also said: " *Those who are sinning rebuke in the presence of all...* " *(1 Tim. 5:20)* As for anyone who dislikes this punishment, the Bible has this to say to him: " *Do not correct a scoffer, lest he hate you; Rebuke a wise man, and he will love you.* " *(Prov. 9:8).*

The work of divine grace is not to pamper or to spoil, but to strengthen, to correct, to refine and to lead the soul to God's love.

Punishment can be of benefit in doing this, whereas to spoil the soul by being soft on it, might well ruin it.

The Lord's love which was manifested on the cross, also leads us to the cross.

[14]

WHAT DOES "TO THE JEWS I BECAME LIKE A JEW" MEAN?

Question?

St. Paul said: *"To the Jews I became like a Jew... to those who are under the law, as under the law, that I might win those who are under the law; to those who are without law, as without law (not being without law toward God, but under law toward Christ), that I might win those who are without law;" (1 Cor. 9:20-21).* **What do these words mean?**

Answer:

The apostle was talking about preaching and seeing that the message of the gospel was conveyed. He is saying: the Jew believes in the Law and the Prophets. In order to convince him of the message of Christ, I speak to him as a Jew, about the Law and the Prophets, and any matters contained in them which pertain to Christ. But when it comes to the Greek, and those like them who do not have a law, who do not believe in the Bible or the Prophets, unless I speak to them in their own way. In terms that they will understand, and attract them to the faith by philosophy, I will not win them for Christ.

Likewise, if I were to speak to them about the Prophets, I would not be able to win them for Christ either.

However, the phrase: "To the Jews I became like a Jew", doesn't mean behaving like a Jew, for St. Paul fought against Judaization with all his might.

Some Jews who embraced Christianity wanted to introduce into it some of the Jewish beliefs and practices, such as circumcision, keeping the Sabbath and the festivals, and the lunar calendar, and all that was associated with them in terms of eating and drinking that which was lawful or unlawful, along with the rest of the Jewish rules concerning purity and unclearness. This movement was known by the name of Judaization.

St. Paul in his attacks against the Jews said: " *So let no one judge you in food or in drink, or regarding a festival or a new moon or sabbaths, which are a shadow of things to come, but the substance is of Christ.* " *(Col. 2:16-17)*.

The words 'in food or in drink' here does not mean fasting, but refers to the purity or impurity of food, according to the foods that were allowed or forbidden in Judaism, but which did not apply any more under Christianity.

St. Paul preached among the Jews, just as he did among the Gentiles. In his sermon in Rome, he spoke first to the Jews. When they rejected him and became divided, he then went to the Gentiles. *(Acts 28:17-29)*.

In order to win the Jews, he spoke in the Temple and in the Jewish synagogues, and tried to convince them of what was said in the Law and the Prophets about Christ.

[15]

HOW TO DEAL WITH PROBLEMS

Question?

How to deal with Problems?.

Answer:

Every human being in the world faces problems in his life. The way in which people deal with such problems, react to them, or let themselves be affected by them, varies. This depends on the personality and the mental attitude of each individual, and also on his experience... There are some types of people who are just crushed by their problems, while others triumph over them. There are also right ways and wrong ways of approaching them. I shall try to consider both kinds:

1. Running away from problems:

The way of escape was that followed by our ancestors Adam and Eve, when they fell into sin. The Bible says: *"they hid from the Lord God among the trees of the garden."* *(Gen. 3:8).*

This running away, however, did not solve the problem, they still had to face it.

Another way in which people react to their problems is with:

2. Unhappiness and tears:

A child's way of facing a difficulty is to cry.

This childish behaviour, though, remains in some people even after they are grown up, and this is frequently the case with women, who then show a tendency to confront any difficulty with unhappiness and crying, without attempting to find any kind of practical solution.

This was the case with St. Hannah when God had closed her womb, so that when her rival Peninnah taunted her, Hannah " *did not eat* " *(1 Sam. 1:7)*.
Yet her depression, tears and refusal to eat did not solve her problem until in the end she took refuge in God.

What happened to St. Hannah also happened to an important king like Ahab.

When Naboth the Jezreelite refused to give him the vineyard, the Bible says: *"Ahab went home, sullen and displeased " (1 Kin. 21:4)*. However, that depression did not solve Ahab's problem, but rather led to a solution in which his wife, Queen Jezebel, intervened to provide him with a practical way of dealing with it - being wrong one - as we shall see...
Many wives resort to unhappiness and tearfulness in trying to solve their problems.

For instance, a husband might go home to find his wife in floods of tears, perhaps for some trivial reason, so he tries to solve the problem, but then she goes on to cry for some other reason, and then for a third. Hence crying becomes her fixed line of action in dealing with anything that opposes her desires. To accompany the tears there are her complaints, and depression, and making a crisis out of everything. All of this tends to make the husband despair of this domestic situation, and want to escape from the house with all its gloom. Thus the woman causes harm to him, and also to herself, and all without achieving any positive result!

3. Pressure and insistence:

A person might have a desire which he wishes to fulfil by any method, but finds opposition to it from his father or mother or boss, so he keeps on insisting on having what he wants, and putting pressure on them in a way that he thinks will lead to their consent in the end.

Delilah used this kind of insistence with Samson, until he revealed his secret to her! She kept asking him to reveal his secret, and each time he eluded her by not telling her the truth. But she persevered in putting pressure on him and then chided him saying: " *How can you say, 'I love you,' when your heart is not with me? You have mocked me these three times, and have not told me where your great strength lies.*" *And it came to pass, when she pestered him daily with her words and pressed him, so that his soul was vexed to death, that he told her all his heart, ... " (Judg. 16:15-17).*

This kind of nagging or insistence might lead to someone giving their consent reluctantly, and without really wanting to.

The surprising thing is, though, that the person who has the desire rejoices at this consent, without caring whether the person who has given this assent really approves of it in ' his heart, or whether he resents having to give it. The Israelites urged God to appoint a king for them, though He was not in favour of this desire, and considered it a rejection of Himself *(1 Sam. 8:7)*. Nevertheless, He yielded to their insistence and gave them a king, against His own wishes. That king was Saul, *'and the Spirit of the Lord departed from Saul'(1 Sam. 16:14)*.

Potiphar's wife tried to force the righteous Joseph to make love to her, but he fled from her *(Gen. 39:10),* and as a result of her attempted seduction, Joseph had to suffer banishment and years in prison. It also resulted, however in this woman having a bad reputation for generations. Thus is a case where insistence brought a very unhappy result!

The Jews pressed Pilate to crucify Christ.

Although he tried in every way to escape ,from their urging, they just put even more pressure on him. He told them that he found no fault in Jesus, that he found Jesus to be a righteous man, and saw no reason to crucify Him. Pilate also asked them if they **really** wanted him to crucify their king?!

To which they replied: *"We have no king but Caesar". When Pilate saw that he could not prevail at all, but rather that a tumult was rising, he took water and washed his hands before the multitude, saying, "I am innocent of the blood of this just Person.... You see to it!" To which the Jews replied:*
"His blood be on us and on our children. " (Matt. 27:24-25)
So the result of their insistence was that the governor gave in to them and ordered Christ to be crucified! Do you imagine that they gained anything from their insistence?!

Some people resort to violence as a way out of their difficulties.

4. Violence:

The prophet David got into a problem with Nabal of Carmel, when the latter refused to give David's troops any food. Thus David decided to solve the problem by force. He girded on his sword and ordered his men to do the same. Then he threatened that by morning not one male who belonged to Nabal would be left alive. *(1 Sam. 25:13 & 22)*.

Was David's method right?! No, not at all. Abigail, Nabal's wife, rebuked him for it, for having decided to shed blood and take revenge for himself. And David thanked her for giving him wise advice. *(1 Sam. 25:33)*.

One of the results of David's use of force, was that the Lord didn't permit him to build the Temple, saying to him: " *But God said to me, 'You shall not build a house for My name, because you have been a man of war and have shed blood." (1 Chr. 28:3).*

When Moses used violence to solve a problem between an Egyptian and a Hebrew, by killing the Egyptian *(Ex. 2:12),* God did not use him for some time, but made him spend forty years tending sheep until he had learned to be gentle, and until it could be said of him that: " *Now the man Moses was very humble, more than all men who were on the face of the earth " (Num. 12:3)* It was only after Moses had developed this final character trait that God used him to look after His people.

Peter was wrong when he raised his sword and cut off the ear of the High Priest's servant. When confronted with the problem of his Master's arrest, Peter thought of solving it by violence, but the Lord rebuked him saying: *"Put your sword back in its place... for all who take the sword will perish by the sword " (Matt. 26:52).*

A father can also fall into the mistake of being violent when he exercises his authority with force at home, and beats his wife or children and causes them harm. This could be true of the priest too, who uses the authority he possesses to excommunicate or ban, in the wrong situation.

5. Trickery and Cunning:

Rebekah used this method so that her favourite son, Jacob. could receive the blessing of his father Isaac.

She clothed Jacob in a goatskin so that his body would seem hairy, like that of his brother Esau *(Gen. 27)*. Isaac, not noticing the trick, bestowed his blessing on Jacob. But do you think Jacob benefited when he deceived his father in this way?- No, he didn't, rather the opposite, for he lived as a fugitive, in fear of his brother Esau, and later became himself a victim of deception, when his uncle, Laban, married him to Leah, instead of Rachel *(Gen. 29:25),* and also changed his wages ten times *(Gen. 31:41).*

Jacob was also deceived by his sons, when they informed him that Joseph had been killed by a wild beast. *(Gen. 37:33)* And in the end, Jacob summed up his life story saying: "*My years have been few and evil...* " *(Gen. 47:9).*

Jezebel used a method of cunning in order to acquire the vineyard of Naboth the Jezreelite. She contrived to get a malicious charge against Naboth and it was announced that he had blasphemed against God, and then brought false witnesses to testify to it. So Naboth was taken outside the city and stoned, and thus Ahab inherited Naboth's vineyard. It appeared that the trick had brought a solution to the problem, but God sent His word to Elijah the Prophet, to say to Ahab: " *Have you murdered and also taken possession?*" ' *And you shall speak to him, saying, 'Thus says the LORD: "In the place where dogs licked the blood of Naboth, dogs shall lick your blood, even yours.* ' " *(1 Kin. 21:17-19).* This also turned out to be the fate of Ahab's wife, Jezebel. *(2 Kin. 9:36).*

Cunning - like violence - may lead to a swift result, and appear to be a solution to a particular problem, but it isn't from God.

God may permit the defeat of such evil plots, just as he brought Ahithophel's advice to nothing, so that it was not able to harm David *(2 Sam. 17..23)*. Thus David was saved, but Ahithophel hung himself out of grief that his advice had failed.

6. Does committing a crime solve the problem?

Some people resort to committing a crime in order to solve their problems, or to attain their goals. This was what Cain, the first killer on earth, did. What was the result? The result was that he lived the rest of his life in fear and terror, as a wanderer and fugitive on earth, afraid that anyone who found him would kill him *(Gen. 4:14)*.

Absalom also resorted to crime when he set fire to Joab's field so that he could meet the king *(2 Sam. 14:30)*.

7. The weapon of betrayal:

Some people resort to "the weapon of betrayal" in order to achieve their objectives. Absalom betrayed his father, David, in order to try and take over the rulership, but his treachery only led to his own death *(2 Sam. 18:15)*. Likewise, when Judas resorted to betrayal, he did not gain from doing so, but ended up hanging himself *(Matt. 27:5)*.

Even though betrayal has brought a certain satisfaction to some people, or has achieved their goal - most often something really mean or base - they have nevertheless all failed, and ended up despising themselves.

While a person might be able to bear the contempt of others towards him, he is rarely able to bear his self-disgust! When the reality of his inner self is revealed to the traitor, he despises it and it becomes unbearable.

Yet in spite of all this, the weapon of betrayal still exists. How easy it is for the traitor to achieve his goal by deceiving his loved ones, or his benefactors, or by betraying a friend if he feels he is a rival... even so, it leads to nothing.

8. Trying to solve problems by nervousness:

Suppose a highly-strung person comes across a problem, and wonders how to solve it. He might try to confront the matter with shouting, causing a fuss, by getting angry or uptight, by swearing, making threats or promises, by using a sharp, loud voice and harsh tones. But none of this can solve his problem.

Getting into a state of nervous agitation is a dissatisfactory means.

It indicates a lack of strategy, a failure to convince or discuss with others, and an attempt to cover up this failure with an outer show of force, which bears witness to an inner incapacity. Or it could be a way of trying to strike fear into the other party, or to get rid of him by this method. It is not, however, a spiritual method, nor is it a socially respectable one, and the difficulty is still there just the same...

It may bring on the person who is like this, various health disorders, such as high blood pressure, nervous tension or stomach ulcers, or diabetes etc., as well as other psychological problems, and can cause many complications in social relationships, as the person attempts to rectify the harmful results of his anger and its effect on other people, but finds no solution.

9. Resorting to drugs and such like:

Another type of person, when facing a problem which he can't seem to solve, may resort to drugs, to the various sorts of tranquillisers, sedatives and sleeping pills, such as Valium, Librium etc. To this category of persons we can also add those who imagine that they can solve their difficulties by alcohol and getting drunk, by smoking or taking barbiturates or illegal drugs.

A person cannot solve his problems by these kinds of drugs, or smoking. He is only trying to distract himself, which isn't a **solution** to his problem, but rather an escape from it. The problem is still there...

Resorting to such drugs is an admission of defeat in facing the difficulty, a failure to bear it, and a failure to solve it. And since it doesn't produce a positive result, the person taking drugs finds the problem just the same, as the effects of the drugs wear off. He may then try to increase his dose, which likewise brings no result, thus he ends up nervously exhausted and in despair until, that is, he attempts to reach a beneficial practical solution.

Some people may try to solve their problems another way, which is:

10. Breaking off friendships and having arguments:

When such a person's social relationships fail, he resorts to breaking off his friendships and starting arguments, to hostility and causing division. This is what happened to Jeroboam when he failed to reach an understanding with Rehoboam. The ten tribes split up and made themselves into independent kingdoms *(1 Kin. 12)*. This division lasted for many centuries, and was not a solution to the problem but rather made the matter worse. The same thing happened between the Jews and the people of Samaria, and also between the Jews and Gentiles... and Jesus Christ came to heal this unsolved problem, and repair relationships between the two people.

But what about you? Do you resort to this course?

11. Confronting the difficulty with lies:

What a lot of people, when facing a problem, try to solve it by lying, or making things up which are not true. They imagine that lying will cover up the problem! when the matter is exposed, they cover up the lie with another, and so on and so forth.. Lying creates an atmosphere of distrust, and the problem gets more complicated.

Another distorted way of approaching problems is by:

12. Being obstinate and rigid-minded:

Such a person, on meeting a difficulty, insists on having his opinion, his point of view, regardless of the awful and disastrous consequences that might follow, and this may change the situation to one of a stubborn impasse and make it even more involved.

All this arises from inner pride, and over-reliance on self. Obstinacy never achieves a good result, because it is an attempt to force the other party, and if that party does not give in, then a clash is inevitable.

The way to deal with this is to try and reach a mutual understanding, and to give up any erroneous fixed attitude.

There is, however, a way which is the complete opposite of obstinacy, and equally wrong, which is that of:

13. Fear and submission:

Some people, when they are hard pressed and feel an inner inadequacy, submit to their particular situation, and passively take whatever happens to them. But this is not a solution to the problem, but just a surrender to it.

If all these methods of facing problems are wrong, what then are the right ways?

The Right ways to Deal with Problems are;

A. Firstly, try to solve the problem by wisdom and intelligence:

Not by 'nerves', or obstinacy or making yourself nervously ill. Do it by wisdom and, as the Bible says, with: *"meekness of wisdom."* *(James 3:13)* It says in Ecclesiastes: *"The wise man's eyes are in his head, But the fool walks in darkness."* *(Eccl. 2:14)*.

In case some people might protest at this by saying that not everyone is wise, and not everyone has this gift, the reply to that is:

B. Seek advice and get the opinion of those who are wise and have experience:

Where the individual is not content with his own opinion, knowledge or experience, he can supplement it with the opinion of his elders.

Another successful method of solving problems is:

C. Prayer and Fasting:

What the individual is incapable of solving, is very easy for God to solve. And prayer and fasting are two ways of bringing God into one's difficulties.

The Bible is full of stories about God solving problems, and the success of the means of fasting and prayer. Queen Esther and her people resorted to this, and so did the people of Ninevah. Likewise David, the prophet, took refuge in his psalms and fasts, and so did Nehemiah, who said: " *when I heard these words, that I sat down and wept, and mourned for many days; I was fasting and praying before the God of heaven." (Neh. 1:4).*

To be truthful, though, we ought to put prayer as the foremost of our means, before wisdom and seeking advice, or a combination of the two together. For the Bible teaches us first of all to pray, just as it tells us to be wise and seek advice.

But there is still another important matter which is:

D. The need to be patient and give the problem time to be solved:

This means patience until God arranges the solution of the problem, at the time which He considers appropriate. For anyone who does not wait patiently, will end up in a state of constant anxiety and nervous exhaustion. Furthermore, in all these things, for a problem to be solved, yet another factor is required, which is:

E. Calmness:

This is necessary because no-one can solve his problems when he is upset.

Calm, peaceful nerves give scope for correct thinking, while an upset state exhausts the soul and paralyses thought, so that the person does not know what to do.

Then it remains to solve the problem by effective and positive action, it can't be done just by wishful thinking.

[16]

ACTING QUICKLY OR TAKING ONE'S TIME

Question?

Which is better: to act swiftly, which indicates resolution, decisiveness, and the ability to make a decision, or to take one's time and deliberate calmly, with all that this conveys in the way of composure, stability and patience?

Answer:

There are cases when it is right and necessary to act swiftly, and others, calling for deliberation and patience, where to act quickly would be harmful...

Take punishment, for example: when this is carried out too quickly, no scope is provided for investigation, for justice, or for close examination, or for finding out the extent of the offence or the position of responsibility. Thus acting quickly in the case of punishment is a mistake, for the matter needs reflection.

On the other hand, being slow and delaying to carry out punishment affords the offender a respite, so that he continues to do wrong, which has worse consequences, in that it encourages others to imitate him, under the impression that there is no form of control or restraint. In such a case, it becomes necessary to carry out a punishment more quickly.

In either case, then, wisdom and an assessment of the circumstances is essential.

It also appears that a thorough investigation is necessary, and that even when swift action in punishment is required, it needs to be accompanied by sufficient justice, and the person to be punished has to be given a chance to explain his situation and answer to his charge.

There are other cases, however, which should be dealt with quickly, such as repentance.

When the prodigal son woke up to his predicament, he said: "*I will arise and go to my father ...* " *(Luke 15:18)* and he got up straightaway and returned to his father. When it comes to repentance, there should be no delay or procrastination. By the time the five foolish maidens returned, they were too late, and found the door closed against them, and their opportunity was lost.

There are situations involving others which, if one is too slow, on the pretext of being deliberate and making a careful examination, will be over and done with by the time one arrives.

Take a sick person, for example, if you catch him in time, and treat him promptly, he might be cured. If you delay ' though, on the excuse that you need to carry out more investigations, his condition might end up as hopeless. You have to do the necessary tests, but do them quickly.

So many times there have been wrongdoers whom we have been too slow to check, with the result that their offence has become a common habit, and spread. And so many situations have reached such serious consequences as someone renouncing his faith, all because we have been too slow to deal with them.

Certain family problems and certain financial problems call for swift action.

There have been situations which have ended up in divorce, which could have been prevented, if steps had been taken to deal with them right at the beginning, before letting them develop into conflicts and become more complicated, and letting them then get to a state of impasse or hatred, and then the law courts and a hearing...

Carrying out obligations often calls for swift action.

Suppose you are a person who is slow in expressing his condolences or his congratulations, or in visiting the sick, or responding on any important occasions, this procrastination might lead to a change in the other person's feelings towards you, so that he imagines that you do not care about him, and so it has an effect on both sides of your relationship.

If you are also slow in making up with him, you might afterwards find yourself no longer on his list of friends!

This does not mean, however, that swift action is best in every situation, and for everybody...

It is a necessary condition, when it comes to carrying out something quickly, that it shouldn't be done in an unprepared or improvisatory manner, or as a reaction. Nor should there be any likelihood of error, or need for re-examination afterwards. For if this were the case, there would be a reason to slow down and not act so quickly.

More important than the factor of speed, is that of skill and usefulness, for if speed is combined with skilful performance, then that is ideal.

What is meant by speed is not recklessness or impetuosity. It is not loss of balance, or behaving without thinking or without prior study, which would not only be wrong, but would also cause extensive damage.

From this, then, the importance of reflection and calmness in producing the right decision, becomes obvious.

Taking consideration over, or reflecting upon a matter, is not an inability to issue a decision, or an inability to make up one's mind in settling affairs, but rather an effort to blend everything with a wise course of behaviour. Calm thinking is more wholesome, and calm behaviour a more successful approach to dealing with something. Calm measures are more lasting and less prone to be shaken...

The surgeon's scalpel, for all its swiftness, is not always the ideal solution.

Between swift action and slowness, there exists, however, a better medium.

Swift action will be criticised, unless it has been backed up by prior study and investigation. And taking one's time about something, doesn't mean just putting things off... it too must be the outcome of deliberation...

Patience is a virtue if it leads to a healthy result, but if I don't use it in the proper place, someone else's more appropriate qualities will gain the advantage!

Acting slowly is not always to be associated with a gentle or peaceable nature, it may sometimes be related to negligence, indifference or stupidity.

Be wise, then, in how you behave, and do not follow either extremes. Taking the middle course has saved many people, and the best way, as they say, is often an intermediate position between two opposite extremes, between overdoing it and underdoing it.

Give each activity its proper time, and deal with each issue in a way that will bring it to success, with swift action, or calm deliberation as is necessary.

[17]

IN PRIVATE OR IN PUBLIC

Question?

Is it better for us to correct people in public or in private if they have fallen into a doctrinal or theological error? And similarly, is it better for a punishment to be carried out in private or in public if someone has done something that requires punishment?

Answer:

The sin that is done in public, punish in public. And the theological error which is broadcast openly in public, should be publicly refuted.

And conversely, those mistakes which are made in private, or theological errors which a person might fall into without anyone else knowing about it, can all be dealt with or punished in private, because they have not spread in society.

But what is the wisdom in all this? Why punish in public, and why correct in public?

This is because something that happens in public has an effect on others, or might cause them to stumble... So we must take those other people into account.

For punishment in public does not confine the wrong to the offender alone, but makes it go beyond him to have an effect on others, who might have imitated that person's action, or who might not have regarded it as serious, or who might have treated it lightly, if it had been allowed to pass unpunished or uncensored. St. Paul said to his disciple Timothy the Bishop concerning this:

" Those who are sinning rebuke in the presence of all, that the rest also may fear." (1 Tim. 5:20).

If, for example, it happened that some people caused a disturbance or an outcry in church, they ought to be reprimanded in front of everyone, as the apostle says, because of the stumbling block it might present to others so that they might not be tempted to do likewise and so that the congregation should learn from it. This matter is different from the personal error which no-one knows about, which our Lord was referring to when He said:

" Moreover if your brother sins against you, go and tell him his fault between you and him alone. " (Matt. 18:15).

As far as a common error is concerned, by which I mean a fault that is widespread, that should also be punished before everybody. Many are the examples of this kind of public punishment with which God corrected His people, or which the prophets and apostles issued to offenders.

And according to the same logic, we can speak about wrong teaching, for to keep silent about teaching that is unorthodox, or inaccurate, especially if it spreads, may cause some people to believe it, since they have not found any way of refuting it.

It might also cause people to become confused with regard to the Church, and start wondering how it, the church, can be quiet about an incorrect teaching that is gaining ground, whether it is through books, magazines or newspapers!

They would then consider the Church has failed in performing its educational function. History presents us with an endless succession of images concerning the stand taken by the Church with regard to theological errors.

The Church used to set up local councils and ecumenical councils to combat theological errors, and this was done in public before everybody.

Whenever doctrinal and theological errors venture forth and take on an openly public form, without showing any consideration for any control or censorship from the Church, then they have to be refuted publicly, as a way of saving those who have become caught up in these ideas, and also to restrain on the originators of those thoughts, by preventing them from making further mistakes, which is what would happen if they found that the Church took no notice of, or was silent about, the errors that were being spread.

The Church also receives many complaints against any unorthodox or strange ideas that spread, and those making the complaints expect to receive an answer.

The Church ought not to remain silent while it sees the potential stumbling block there, in front of her, and ought not simply to take no notice when faced with the people's complaints, especially if they happen again and again and increase in number. For the Church will then find itself facing a duty which it has to perform...

We, as individuals, may have to relinquish our personal right to retaliate or reply, if some people hurt us as individuals, but when it comes to performing our duty to teach, or to protect the faith, then we certainly cannot give in and let any abuse pass by unchallenged.

St. Paul publicly reprimanded St. Peter, when the latter was in the wrong, and what is more, he opposed him face to face *(Gal. 2:11)*.

This was in spite of the fact that Peter, one of the pillars of the Church, who had been given the right hand of fellowship *(Gal. 2:9)*, was a more senior apostle than Paul. And Peter was also one of those to whom Paul had presented his gospel (by which I mean the preaching which he delivered to the Gentiles) *(Gal. 2:2)*. But when Paul saw Peter and those with him doing wrong, " *And the rest of the Jews also played the hypocrite with him, so that even Barnabas was carried away with their hypocrisy.* " *(Gal. 2:13)*, Paul said*:* " *when I saw that they were not straightforward about the truth of the gospel,* **I said to Peter before them all,** *"If you, being a Jew, live in the manner* *of Gentiles and not as the Jews, why do you compel Gentiles to live as Jews? "We who are Jews by nature, and not sinners of the Gentiles,..."(Gal. 2:14-15).*

in matters of belief, the Church does not turn the other cheek, as the Bible tells us to do, that is, it won't sacrifice the correct teaching for the sake of being polite.

When it comes to things that happen in private, or out of the public eye, then the Church does not disclose these but lets them remain unpublished - and there are a good many of such cases.

[18]

CRITICISM AND CONDEMNATION

Question?

What is the difference between criticism and condemnation? And am I, by virtue of my job as a critic, committing a sin by criticising?

Answer:

The basic difference between criticism and condemnation is that criticism is objective, whereas condemnation is something directed towards more personal aspects.

Healthy criticism is a form of analysis, and a process of careful evaluation which highlights good as well as bad points, and gives the subject its full dues, making excuses for any weaknesses if there is scope to do so.

Condemnation which only mentions the bad points, however, is a kind of attack, and anyone doing this is not being just.

Likewise there are various types, and various degrees of criticism, such as calm, serious criticism which has a rational style, and there is biting, spiteful criticism and wounding criticism. Each critic has a different style, and differs in choosing which words he uses. Look and see which kind you are!

Be objective and fair, and do not be harsh in your criticism.

If your official job happens to be that of a critic, then there is nothing wrong in that, sometimes a writer criticises a book and his criticism is all praise for that book, if it deserves it.

Criticism also requires study and knowledge, and has its own principles, and not everyone can ascend to, the rank of a true critic, or can claim this quality for himself.

Readers benefit from the criticism of the scholarly and fair minded critic, and so does the person whom he criticises, and the critic then is contributing to the advancement of literature and scholarship.

[19]

SHOULD THE SACRAMENTS BE SOLD?

Question?

Can the Church Sacraments be sold, so that a price is fixed eg. for baptism, or for the anointing of the sick?

Answer:

The sacraments cannot be sold, because they are derived from the work of the Holy Spirit. And the gifts of the Holy spirit are not to be purchased by money *(Acts 8:20).*

However, if on the occasion of a baptism a person wants to give something to the Church, not as payment but as an offering, like a sacrifice of praise, then a box can be found in the Church for such contributions as these and a person can put in as much as he likes, without anything being demanded from him. And the Church probably cannot tell whether this person has given anything or not, and if it did know that he had put something in the donation box, then it couldn't tell whether it was a large or small sum.

Generally speaking, we encourage baptism as something necessary for salvation *(Mark 16:16),* so it would be unthinkable for the Church to ask for something material in exchange for it...

Furthermore, we strongly invite people to get their children baptised, and criticise them if they are too slow in doing so. We rejoice with them on the day of baptism, because it is on that day that the one being baptised becomes a member of the Church, a member of the body of Christ, and one of the children of God.

If someone on this happy day wishes to make an offering to God, then this is something that springs from that person's heart and feelings.

There is no compulsion or forcing someone to do so, and no fee is charged, God forbid!

We can say the same about the other similar sacraments too.

Take the anointing of the sick, for example, this is an act of love, and is a prayer on behalf of the sick person.

It would be inconceivable for this to become an occasion for raking in money! If it were to, it would lose whatever love and concern it had, and the sick person would not feel the value of a prayer that he had paid for, and which wouldn't be said unless it had been paid for.

If only we would remember always what our Lord said to His disciples: "*Freely you have received, freely give. (Matt. 10:8)*

What is paid to the Church sometimes on certain occasions, is not a fee for the sacrament, but a voluntary offering to the Lord. The sacraments are not for sale: no price can be put on them.

[20]

WHAT DOES 'I HAVE KEPT YOU FROM SINNING AGAINST ME' MEAN?

I was once asked the question:

Question?

What do the words of the Sovereign Lord to Abimelech, when the latter took Abraham's wife, Sarah, mean: " *I also withheld you from sinning against Me; therefore I did not let you touch her."* **(Gen. 20:6) Was this something against the human being's free will?**

Answer:

God has given man freedom, but it is not absolute freedom.

If this freedom is diverted towards something evil, which endangers the eternal life of that person, or someone else, then God can intervene to put a limit to this evil, or to punish the wrongdoer or stop him, and that is because God is the Almighty.

If God were never to restrain on this freedom, but left it alone to do absolutely any evil, it would simply sweep away the poor and weak.

In fact God set a limit to the evil of Satan himself, as is clear in the story of the righteous Job. *(Job 1:12; 2:6)* And in Psalm 125 it also says: *" For the scepter of wickedness shall not rest On the land allotted to the righteous " (Ps. 125:3)* God also intervened to set a limit to Pharaoh's cruelty. And how beautiful are the words in Psalm 12: *" For the oppression of the poor, for the sighing of the needy, Now I will arise," says the LORD; "I will set him in the safety for which he yearns.' " (Ps. 12:5)*.

God gives freedom even to sinners and if they go too far, in such a way that threatens the righteous, then He will intervene to save the righteous and also to establish justice.

There are countless examples of this in the Bible and throughout history and they go to prove God's care and concern.

In the story of Abimelech, though, God intervened out of His grave concern for Sarah's chastity and for the feelings of Abraham, and also to save Abimelech from committing an enormous sin. This was because Abimelech had taken Sarah in all good faith, since Abraham had told him that Sarah was his sister, not his wife. *(Gen. 20:11-12)*.

We do not call this, intervening to limit someone's freedom, but rather intervening in order to save that person from sin. Don't let us forget that Sarah was the wife of a prophet, and from her descendants the Messiah would come!

[21]

SINS ARE NOT EQUAL IN DEGREE, NOR IN PUNISHMENT

Question?

Are sins equal or do they differ in degree? Will the people in Hell all suffer the same punishment? Or are there different degrees of punishment? And which verses of the Bible support this?

Answer:

The Lord said that He would come and " *give to every one according to his work.* " *(Rev. 22:12)* Obviously people's actions differ, and so therefore will their punishment. Even on earth, the Lord said in the Sermon on the Mount: " *And whoever says to his brother, 'Raca!*# *shall be in danger of the council. But whoever says, 'You fool!' shall be in danger of hell fire." (Matt. 5:22).* From this it is clear that punishment differs with the difference in degree of the offence. St. Augustine also made this observation.

Concerning this difference in degree of sin, and the Church's attitude towards it, St. John said: " There is sin leading to death. I do not say that he should pray about that.

An Aramic term of contempt

All unrighteousness is sin, and there is sin not leading to death." (1 John 5:16-17) So, a sin that does not lead to death, can be prayed for, so that the one who has committed it should be given life. Sins which do not lead to death come under the headings of unintentional sins, sins of ignorance and sins of negligence.

Obviously there is a great difference between the unintentional sin, and the sin which is carried out with full intent and determination. Just as there is a big difference between sins of ignorance and those committed in full knowledge. God's justice requires that the punishment should be in proportion to the crime.

Sins are actually alike in that they exclude one from the Kingdom of Heaven, but even those who go to hell suffer different degrees of torture, which is why the Lord said, referring to all the cities which rejected Him and rejected the faith and rejected His disciples: " *Assuredly, I say to you, it will be more tolerable for the land of Sodom and Gomorrah in the day of judgment than for that city!" (Matt. 10:15)*

The words 'more tolerable... than' prove the difference in punishment based on the difference in offence.

The difference in sin can be clearly observed from the practical point of view. The person who commits adultery in his mind, for instance, is not like the person who commits the act of adultery, for the latter, by doing so, has defiled his own body and that of someone else too. And the person who commits the act of adultery, is not the same as someone who commits a violent rape, which is that much, more offensive. And a different case again would be that of someone who commits adultery with a relative whom the law has forbidden him to marry. *(Lev. 20)*

A person who wishes to do something violent, but doesn't do it, and just keeps it in his mind, is not the same as someone who actually carries out his violence in physical or verbal form, who actually does harm to another person and, by his action, causes others to stumble. The one who only thinks about stealing, is different from the one who actually steals by force.

At this point, though, sin becomes multiple or compound, which means that it consists of a number of sins together.

The punishment for a multiple sin is greater because it does not rank as a single sin, but as a collection of sins. Someone who insults a person will have committed the sin of insulting, but someone who insults his father or mother, will have added to his sin of insulting, another sin which is that of breaking the commandment to honour your parents. Thus his sin is a compound one, and accordingly his punishment will be harsher. The Bible says in the law of Moses: *"If anyone curses his father or mother, he must be put to death and his blood will be on his own head." (Lev. 20:9)*.

Likewise, someone who hit someone else, to whom he was not related, used to be subject, after being judged, to the rule, *"an eye for an eye; a tooth for a tooth." (Lev. 24:19-20)*. But someone who hit his father or mother used to be stoned and

an even harsher stoning was given for sins committed against anything sacred.

If someone sins on a holy day, such as a day of fasting, for example, or a day of taking communion, is held to have committed a worse sin, therefore the punishment was more severe for the sins of the sons of Eli the Priest *(1 Sam. 2)*.

[22]

THE VIEW OF CHRISTIANITY REGARDING ORGAN TRANSPLANTS

Question?

Is it permissible that an organ of one human being's body (whether it is from a live or dead body) be transplanted into that of another? And would organ transplant constitute meddling around with bodies, and not showing due respect for them? Is it also permissible for a person to give a part of his own body since he does not own it?

Answer:

Christianity does not prohibit organ transplantion, either from a living or a dead body.

The Holy Bible does not expressly instruct on, or forbid, organ transplant, either in the New or in the Old Testament, because that subject was not around at that time. But the spirit of the Bible calls for giving and self-sacrifice, for saving others and for showing as much concern as possible for other people's lives.

So from the teaching of the Bible, organ transplant is permissible, whether from a live body or from a dead one, in order to benefit another human being.

Christianity does not regard that as meddling around with a body that has been given to a person by God, or as doing it harm, or as trying to engineer a new human form, or as violating its dignity.

The body is only destroyed by sin, by harmful habits, by neglecting health rules, suicide or such like.

But to lose a limb through doing a noble deed, such as defending one's country... or to give an organ in order to save a human being in an operation, is a kind of sacrifice, and a giving of oneself for others, which raises the dignity of the human being, and which is in no way contrary to religion.

This is what the martyrs did whether they were martyrs for their homeland or for religion. They submitted their lives to death, and exposed their bodies to being torn apart and mutilated. We honour the martyrs whose limbs were cut to pieces, and whose bodies were disfigured, and we regard their loss of limbs as something that increases their honour, both in the eyes of God and of men. We do not call that a disfiguration of their bodies, but something that adds to their dignity.

To a certain degree, sacrificing organs in order to save people's lives, or donating them after death for the benefit of medicine or science in general, resembles this.

Thus to give an organ of the human body, voluntarily, does not violate the dignity of the body, because the body's dignity is not in its form, but in its being sacrificed for the good of others.

The gospel calls us to sacrifice ourselves, when Jesus said: "*Greater love has no one than this, than to lay down one's life for his friends.*" *(John 15:13)*.

If the Gospel calls for the laying down one's whole life for the sake of others, then there is all the more reason to sacrifice a single organ of the human body.

Our concern that our bodies should be instruments in the service of the spirit, and be fit to accompany it on life's journey, does not mean that we should be driven by selfishness to preserve these bodies at all costs!! No, on the contrary, for in donating a part of the body, the spirit will rise higher.

It says in the Bible that love "*is not self-seeking.* " *(1 Cor. 13:5)*. And St. Paul also said to the Galatians: " *I bear you witness that, if possible, you would have plucked out your own eyes and given them to me.*" *(Gal. 4:15)*. That kind of operation, however, was not possible twenty centuries ago. We hope that science will help to make it possible for such things to be carried out, and that love will help to put them into effect, in the future...

So we can ask what is better;for a human being to live with two kidneys, or for him to give one of them to someone else, and for them both to live? As by this sacrifice and love a

person is helping someone else's life, by rescuing him from death and from the agony of illness.

The same can be said, to a certain extent, about blood transfusion, or transplanting any part of the body to another human being. In the case of a single human being, we might notice that various organs or parts of his body might be given either to him, or by him, in certain operations, for instance - transplanting an artery, a skin, nerve or tissue graft... without anyone raising any objection or disputing the concept.

As far as a dead person is concerned, removing one of his organs will not hurt him, but may well save somebody else's life!

I wonder if a person who doesn't wish to donate any of his organs for the benefit of another person, can stop the worms from eating his dead body?! Do you suppose he can prevent the decay or the decomposition of his body after his death?! And where does all that has been said about the respecting of the human body and not meddling around with it or engineer changes in it, come into all this disintegration?!

In the Bible man was told right from the beginning: " *you shall eat bread Till you return to the ground, For out of it you were taken; For dust you are, And to dust you shall return* " *(Gen. 3:19).* And it also says: " *the dust will return to the earth as it was, and the spirit will return to God who gave it.*" *(Eccl. 12:7).*

Since the body will return to the earth after death, then it is not disrespectful towards any organ of the body to be grafted onto or transplanted into another body, and so continue to have life!

We need have no fear on behalf of the body when it is dead, whatever might happen to its organs, since we all believe in the resurrection of the body after death.

I support the idea of creating an organ bank too and religion is in no way opposed to this concept.

Religion instructs us to do good and what a wonderful thing it is for a person to do good in his life by generously donating an organ, or part of his body that he can live without, or likewise after his death, by promising some of his organs (either through a written instruction such as a will, or by word of mouth) to save others, or for the benefit of science! And that other person who benefited from the transplant might in turn like to repay this favour by instructing that his organs be used after his death to save others.

This is how the cycle of goodness revolves, at the hands of the living and the dead alike, and each will receive a reward from God according to the good he has done to others.

As far as the idea that our bodies are not ours to give away to others is concerned, we can reply to that by saying, that neither are our souls our property, yet we sacrifice them for the sake of others, out of love, or in accordance with the command of religion and it is a virtue for us to do so.

Therefore, we have all the more reason to sacrifice an organ or part of the body.

We can say that our souls are not ours to do away with, through suicide for example, or to ruin by taking drugs.

But to use the body and soul in connection with doing good and benefiting others, is something which religion blesses and which God instructs.

[23]

HOW SHOULD WE PRAY?

Question?

Sometimes when I stand to pray I don't know what to say, or I say a few words and come to a halt. How should I pray, and what should I say?

Answer:

There are many elements to prayer which, if you are aware of them, can help you to lengthen your time in God's presence.

Many people just content themselves with the element of asking, so that they confuse prayer with requesting, with the result that if they have nothing to ask for they do not pray!

Even on the level of asking, though, prayer can be broadened, so that we 'ask' on behalf of others. You can make requests to God for the Church, and for the society in which you live, for all those whom you know who are in need, for each one according to his needs, whether he is sick or in a difficult situation, or travelling or studying.

There is also the element of thanksgiving in prayer. Thank God for all His goodness to you, and to those you know and love, do it in detail. The Church has set down for us the Prayer of Thanksgiving, at the beginning of each section of the prayers of the hours.

There is also in prayer, the element of confession, in which you confess to God your sins and shortcomings, and ask His pardon and forgiveness, just as you ask Him for strength or healing... but do all of this with humility and surrender.

In prayer there is also the elements of praise, glorification and contemplation on the beautiful qualities of God. Take for example the phrase, 'Holy, Holy, Holy, is the Lord God of Hosts. Heaven and earth are full of Your glory', this does not spring from penitence, but from contemplating the attributes of God.

There is some advice I can give you if you feel that you don't know how to pray, which is:

You already have prayers that have been written down, and which you have perhaps learned by heart. The Lord gave us an example of this in the Lord's Prayer, 'Our Father...'. There are also the Psalms and the Agpeya (The name given to the book of prayer settings for the various hours of the day, which is used in the Coptic Orthodox Church), the hymns of praise and the Psalmody.

You can pray from them however you like, they are a teacher to teach you to pray, and to instruct you in the best manner in which to address God, and what to say, how to say it, and how to open your heart to meditate in prayer.

[24]

ABOUT ASKING FOR GIFTS

Question?

Why shouldn't we ask the Lord to give us supernatural gifts, such as speaking in tongues and healing the sick and performing miracles? Doesn't the apostle Paul say: " *desire spiritual gifts"? (1 Cor. 14: 1)* **and "** *earnestly desire the best gifts* **" *(1 Cor. 12:31)*.**

Answer:

The fruits of the Spirit, are more important for you and more beneficial than the gifts of the Spirit.

St. Paul also said about the fruits of the Spirit: " *the fruit of the Spirit is love, joy, peace, longsuffering, kindness, goodness, faithfulness, gentleness, self-control. Against such there is no law." (Gal. 5:22-23).*

These fruits are of advantage to your eternal life, which is why the apostle calls them 'the most excellent way', when he says: " *earnestly desire the best gifts. And yet I show you a more excellent way." (1 Cor. 12:31).*

He explains how love is the first of the fruits of the Spirit, superior to speaking in the tongues of men or of angels, better than all knowledge or all mysteries, better than prophecy and better than faith which can move mountains. *(1 Cor. 13:1-3)*.

He said that prophecies will cease, tongues will be stilled, and knowledge will pass away, but that love will remain, and that it is greater than faith and hope.

As for miracles, they do not necessarily redeem the soul. Many of those who have done miracles have perished, and likewise miracles have been attributed to Satan and his followers.

Look at what the Lord said in His Sermon on the Mount: " *Many will say to Me in that day, 'Lord, Lord, have we not prophesied in Your name, cast out demons in Your name, and done many wonders in Your name?'* "*And then I will declare to them, 'I never knew you; depart from Me, you who practice lawlessness!'(Matt. 7:22)*

This is quite a surprise! So these people turned out to be evildoers, and they perished, and the Lord refused to recognise them, in spite of the fact that they had driven out demons and prophesied, and attributed it all to the Lord's name!!

When the disciples rejoiced at the miracles they had been enabled to perform, the Lord told them not to do so.

The disciples *"returned with joy and said, 'Lord, even the demons submit to us in Your name.* " But Jesus said to them:
" *do not rejoice in this, that the spirits are subject to you, but*

*rather rejoice because your names are written in heaven."
(Luke 10:20)*

And when He was tempted by the Devil on the mountain, the Lord refused to perform miracles.

He refused to change stones into bread, and refused to throw Himself down from the high place to prove that the angels would bear Him up...- because the Lord didn't wish to perform miracles for pleasure, or for worldly glory. 'So when the Jews asked Him for a sign, He used to say to them: " *An evil and adulterous generation seeks after a sign, and no sign will be given to it except the sign of the prophet Jonah." (Matt. 12:39).* Thus Jesus led them to think about His cross, death and resurrection, rather than the spectacle of miracles or signs.

Wanting gifts, and wanting to perform miracles could be a war by which Satan attacks you and deceives you by gratifying your pride, and then leading you astray.

The Bible says about the Antichrist, the person who deceives, that he is a man of sin, a man doomed to destruction, that he will oppose and exalt himself over everything that is called God, and set himself up in God's temple proclaiming himself to be God, that he will make many go astray, and lead them to apostasy... And it says that: *"The coming of the lawless one will be.. displayed in all kinds of counterfeit miracles, signs and wonders, and in every sort of evil that deceives those who are perishing. " (2 Thess. 2:3-10)*

How easy it is for Satan to lead people astray by miracles, or to lead them to be proud, by deceiving them with false signs.

If Satan sees you as someone who likes visions and dreams, he can appear to you in false visions and dreams... And if he sees you as someone who is keen on casting out demons, he can come out of a person and go back in, and thus play around with you and deceive you into thinking that you are gifted in this kind of work. The Devil is capable of appearing in the form of an angel of light, as the Bible tells us. So if he sees you as someone who likes wonders and marvels, he can fight you from this aspect. You can find examples of this in the book "Paradise of the Monks".

The war of pride, however, can arise even with real miracles.

Look at St. Paul, a giant of a figure in the Church, and see how he says: "*And lest I should be exalted above measure by the abundance of the revelations, a thorn in the flesh was given to me, a messenger of Satan to buffet me, lest I be exalted above measure.(2 Cor. 12:7).* God must have considered that affliction was beneficial to Paul, and so did not agree to the Apostle's prayer to remove it from him.

So if even St. Paul himself was wary of these miracles, lest they. should make him think too highly of himself, shouldn't you be wary too?!

"Do not be haughty but fear." (Rom. 11:20), as Paul says, though he goes on in fact to give you further advice which applies to all people in regard to spiritual gifts:

" not to think of himself more highly than he ought to think, but to think soberly, as God has dealt to each one a measure of faith.(Rom. 12:3).

Why do you think more highly of yourself than you ought? Why do you ask for the performance of miracles, something which not even one of the saints, asked for? Why don't you concern yourself with the fruits of the Spirit rather than the gifts?

Is it not sometimes a war of pride that deceives you into asking for gifts? Verse *"desire spiritual gifts. "* **(1 Cor. 14:1) however, does not mean that you have to ask for them.**

It means, rather, that you should make your heart worthy to be given them. God cannot give you miraculous powers unless you are humble, because only the humble person is properly cautious about miracles.

Humility does not demand, miracles but receives them with a feeling of not having deserved them, while accepting that the Lord in His wisdom must have performed them because He deemed it beneficial to His creation in some way.

John the Baptist was the greatest man ever born of woman, yet he wasn't famous for performing miracles, nor did he ask to perform them. `

[25]

THE HIGHEST VIRTUE OF ALL

Question?

What is the highest virtue of all?.

Answer:

The virtue which encompasses all virtues is that of love since on love depend all the Law and the Prophets.

But the basis of all the virtues, the basis on which every good work is built, is the virtue of humility, because every virtue that is not based on humility can lead to self-righteousness and false glory, by which the individual can perish.

Even love itself, which is the greatest virtue, can cause man to perish, if it is not built on humility. In this case it couldn't actually be called 'love', in the exact meaning of the word.

[26]

FOLLOWING THE LIVES OF THE SAINTS

Question?

Whenever I read books of the lives of the saints my soul starts to yearn to become like them, though unfortunately I am unable to do as they did. What would you advise?.

Answer:

Many of those who have written about the examples of the saints have mentioned practices which the saints attained - perhaps only after decades of struggle - without having mentioned the exercises which they practised, or the gradual steps which they followed until they reached that level.

Do you want, just by reading, and just in one sudden leap, to perform what it took the saints years and years to attain?!

Put excellence before you, by all means, but remember that you need two things to reach it:

a) a step by step approach.
b) spiritual guidance.

And you also need to look at a third point which is, how that particular virtue is suitable for you personally in your kind of life, which might be quite different from the kind of life of the saint whom you are reading about.

For example, silence and constant prayer are suited to the life of seclusion, but are difficult to practise when one has to mix in the company of other people. If a person were to try, to carry them out in such circumstances, he would certainly fall into practical difficulties, and perhaps clash with others.

Similarly, very strict or total fasting, is something more suitable for those who live a solitary life, than for those who have to make greater physical efforts, or those who are young and still growing.

Generally speaking, in your spiritual practices you are supposed to be under the guidance of a wise and experienced father, not following your own whims, because those who have no guide, fall like the leaves of the trees.

Your guide will protect you from going to extremes, and from getting too fanatical, or being excessive, and from making sudden leaps which don't have a secure basis.

So do not be sad, then, if you cannot do now what the saints used to do. Perhaps you will later on, but you will only get there one step at a time, by gradual development.

We also notice how every saint had his own particular virtue which he possessed, but are you wanting to possess all the virtues of all the saints put together - something which would be very rare indeed?! Keep a sense of proportion!

[27]

WHETHER IT IS NECESSARY TO KNOW HOW TO READ AND WRITE IN ORDER TO BE A MONK OR A NUN

Question?

I am a young woman aged 23, who does not know how to read and write, though I know how to sew and embroider. Is it possible for me to become a nun or is monasticism only open to those who have been to school and can read and write?.

Answer:

Anyone can enter the monastic life, whether educated or not. It depends on renouncing the world, dedicating oneself to worship and prayer, training in the life of holiness and purity of heart, along with losing one's life in terms of this world... But what is important, as far as you are concerned, is how you pray, and how you spend your time.

Perhaps you don't have the capacity yet for constant prayer and deep prayers of the heart, that occupy your whole time.

The **Agpeya** prayer book, along with the prayers of the saints, can help you to fill your time with prayer. But how can you learn the Psalms and the prayers of the prayer book without knowing how to read or write?

The only thing you could do would be to get someone to teach you all these psalms and prayers, so that you could memorise them, just as the teachers of the Church hymns are responsible to pass them on to others. But this would have to be before joining a monastic order.

We can also say the same about the hymns of praise which the nuns recite in church after the midnight prayer. This requires a reading and writing knowledge of the Coptic language, not only Arabic.

A certain amount of time in the monastic life is spent in reading the Bible and spiritual books, the lives of the saints and other useful books.

Reading is not only something to occupy your time, but is so that you can gain from the spiritual thoughts, feelings, meditations and love for goodness which certain writings can inspire in the heart.

You will miss out on all this if you do not know how to read and write, and I don't just mean that you will lose something by not being familiar with them as knowledge, but you will not be able to enjoy the benefits of their effect on your spiritual life.

Your not knowing how to read or write might perhaps create within you inferiority complex, especially if you compare yourself to the other nuns who do have this spiritual potential.

But does all this mean that you should abandon the idea of entering the religious life for these reasons, or could we look for a remedy? The answer might be for you to put an end to your illiteracy, as now there are schools established for this purpose.

Or the remedy might be for you to learn the Psalms and prayers and parts of the Agpeya, plus the tunes of the Psalmody, and begin memorising them straightaway, just as the specialist teachers in the Church memorise them.

You can also train yourself to pray from the heart, or to pray continuously or repeat short prayers or special prayers, so that you will not lose the essential element of prayer, which is the basis of the monastic life.

Try to compensate for your inability to read, by some other means, such as by endeavouring to apply yourself to the element of prayer by memorising and training yourself to do it.

If a person is serious about his spiritual life, and in his orientation towards the religious life, even if he is illiterate, he can gain a great deal from the readings in the Church which are taken from the Books of the Bible and the Synaxarium (the history of saints celebrated by the Coptic

Church), along with listening to what his fellows in the monastic order recite.

The Bible can be recorded on cassette tapes to be listened to. Although this is rather a hard way to learn, it leads to good results, in that it is better than being deprived for ever of reading the Bible, or listening to it whenever one wants.

All this applies if one is steadfast about joining this order and his purpose is wholly dedicated to that. The life of one seeking to join monasticism needs to be holy in God's eyes, pleasing to the other monks or nuns in the monastery and meet the approval of the director in charge.

The monastic life is not just learning and knowledge. There are those who make up for a lack of knowledge, with purity of the heart, just as some of the saints did.

If, however, there is ignorance of the spiritual life, in addition to an inability to read and to write, then it would be better to abandon the idea of embarking on monasticism.

[28]

THE MEEK WILL INHERIT THE EARTH

Question?

What does *"Blessed are the meek, for they will inherit the earth"(Matt. 5:5)* **mean?** .

Answer:

The meek person is someone who is quiet, kind and simple, who does not quarrel or shout - you never hear his voice raised in the street. He keeps well away from arguments conflicts and lengthy disputes. He is peaceable, doesn't insist on his own way, is considerate and kind hearted, he gets on well with people and has a sensitive nature and a friendly smile.

These qualities make him popular and loved by all. And because of this - in addition to inheriting the kingdom of God - he inherits the earth, since those who dwell on earth love him, and he lives with them in peace and tranquillity.

St. Augustine, however, interpreted the phrase, 'will inherit the earth', to mean 'the land of the living', according to what it says in *Psalm 27 (v. 13)*: *"I will see the goodness of the Lord in the*

Land of the living. " This 'land of the living' is what St. John the Visionary spoke about when he said: *"Now I saw a new heaven and a new earth. " (Rev. 21:1),* and it symbolises the land which overflows with milk and honey.

[29]

FREE TIME

Question?

How should a young person occupy his free time especially during the summer holidays?.

Answer:

Having free time, or spare time, and not knowing what to do in it, is a problem that needs to be dealt with, because anyone who is conscious of having nothing to do, is someone who, on one hand doesn't know the value of time, and on the other, doesn't know the way to occupy that time in a useful way.

There are two ways of occupying spare time: either for the benefit of the person himself, who has that free time, or in the service of those around him and for their benefit.

Occupying the time for the benefit of the person himself could be by reading or study, in order to increase his knowledge or education, and extend his mental faculties, always providing that he chooses the kind of reading that will benefit him in this way.

An individual might benefit from taking up various interests, or practising certain hobbies, according to his talents, or spending his spare time acquiring new and useful skills, or learning something practical, either at home or at an institution, or from friends or advisers.

A young person might take part in any sporting activity to strengthen his body as long as this does not consume all his time.

But what a nice thing it is for someone to occupy his spare time in spiritual service, or in social work for the benefit of others! In serving others, he also benefits at the same time.

Besides this there are tasks which the Church can provide to fill young people's free time, in a programme designed for their benefit. This could be by taking an interest in visual or oral aids to instruction, setting up meetings for discussion, organising parties and lectures, and various means of entertainment, which convey a spiritual benefit at the same time.

Interest must be shown, and efforts made to set up clubs and libraries of religious books, to develop constructive ways of using young people's spare time and energies in a way that benefits them, and helps their talents to develop, while sharing in carrying out projects for the Church and participating in its activities.

[30]

EVERYONE WHO HAS WILL BE GIVEN MORE

Question?

What is the meaning of the verse: " *'For to everyone who has, more will be given, and he will have abundance; but from him who does not have, even what he has will be taken away.* **"** *(Matt. 25:29)* **What does it mean that one does not have yet it will be taken from him?**

Answer:

It means that to anyone who has faith, and a love for doing good work, or to anyone who does good, God will give a blessing, in order to increase that person's faith or good works, or both.

But anyone who does **not** have faith, and whose actions are carried out **without** faith, will have those actions taken away from him, and they will have no value because they were not done in faith.

The same goes for a person who doesn't do good works, and whose faith is without works, to which one could apply the words: "*Faith by itself, if it does not have works, is dead.*" *(James 2:17)* This 'dead' faith will be taken away from that person. This faith which is just in name, or just something intellectual, or formal, will be taken away from him.

[31]

THE REAL ELEMENTS OF STRENGTH

Question?

I want to have a strong personality. What are the elements of strength of character by which I can become strong?

Answer:

The apostle St. John said: "*I have written to you, fathers, Because you have known Him who is from the beginning. I have written to you, young men, Because you are strong, and the word of God abides in you, And you have overcome the wicked one.*" *(1 John 2:14).*

So, the strong person is one who has overcome evil, because the word of God lives in him. A leader great enough to defeat an enemy's army and conquer cities, can be defeated by his lust, and thus is not necessarily truly strong. This is why the wise man says, 'He who conquers himself is better than he who conquers a city'.

This is the spiritual strength by which a person can defeat his passions and lusts, and can also lead others spiritually.

There is another kind of strength of character which arises from certain qualities in the personality, such as intelligence, wisdom, being well-organised, and able to win people's hearts, having a good memory, being energetic and full of vitality. A person's real strength springs from within him, from his victory over himself, from his influence on others, from his strong relationship with God, from his talents, and good behaviour. It might also come from his success, or from his ability to do productive work in various different fields.

Strength is not a false outer appearance of power, nor is it an authority that springs from rank or official position or from wealth.

[32]

IF YOUR EYE OR HAND CAUSES YOU TO SIN

Question?

Is it right for a person to gouge his eye out, or cut off his hand, if it causes him to sin, as the Bible prescribes? (Matt. 5:29-30).

Answer:

The Lord meant to stress the need to keep well away from anything that might cause one to stumble, as he said: "*for it is more profitable for you that one of your members perish, than for your whole body to be cast into hell.*" *(Matt. 5:30).*

This commandment, however, ought not to be taken literally, but for its spiritual meaning. It would be very difficult if it were literal!

Some of the saints, though, carried out this commandment literally, such as Simon Al-Kharaz, and some women saints who are mentioned in the book 'Bustan Al-Ruhban' [Paradise of The Monks].

But it would be impossible, and impracticable for this commandment to be carried out literally, as a general rule, otherwise the majority of people in the world would be one-eyed or one-handed, because our eyes and hands cause us to sin or stumble so often, especially at a certain age, and in particular circumstances and situations.

Many of the saints, however, interpreted one's 'eye' in this context to mean the person who is most dear to oneself, and one's 'hand' they interpreted to mean the person who is most helpful to one. So that if either one of them should cause you to sin, you must cut yourself off from their close association.

We also observe that in some of its canon laws the Church has forbidden the cutting off of parts of the human body, if one is afraid that they might cause one to sin; for example, there is the law which bans castration of oneself.

In any case, literally cutting off the hand or gouging out the eye, does not automatically prevent one from stumbling or sinning, because sin often arises from within the heart.

If the heart is pure, a person can see and will not stumble. So it is better to take this command in its spiritual sense, rather than literally.

Another case where this needs to be stressed concerns what our Lord said in Mark's gospel: *"It is better for you to enter life maimed, ... lame, ... with one eye , ... than to be cast into hell". (Mark. 9:43-47).*

Naturally we shouldn't take these words literally, because a person cannot be 'maimed, lame, or 'one-eyed' in heaven?!

We can't imagine a righteous man in heaven with any kind of deficiency, just as this could not be the reward given to the righteous for their goodness, and for not stumbling, at whatever price... !

The Bible teaches us that *"the letter kills, but the Spirit gives life. " (2 Cor. 3:6)*

Therefore we cannot take all the commandments in the Bible literally. The Lord wanted to show us by this commandment the danger of stumbling into sin, and the need to avoid it, even if it should lead to losing something very precious to oneself.

[33]

SIMPLICITY

Question?

What is to be understood by 'simplicity' in Christianity.

Answer:

Simplicity is, not being complicated, and in Christianity it also means, not being naive.

The Christian can be simple, i.e. straightforward and modest in character, and yet wise at the same time. Christian simplicity is a wise simplicity. Christian wisdom is an uncomplicated wisdom, by which I mean, uninvolved, not abstruse like some philosophies. This is why the Lord said: *"be wise as serpents and harmless as doves. "* *(Matt. 10:16).*

[34]

THE ATTITUDE OF CHRISTIANITY TOWARDS WINE

Question?

What is the doctrine of Christianity regarding wine? Is it allowed or forbidden? Or when is it allowed or forbidden?

Answer:

In answering this question, I would like to put before you three points which are:

1. Christianity does not prohibit the substance as a substance, but rather prohibits the abuse of the substance.

2. Orthodox Christianity distinguishes between wine and intoxicating liquor or spirits, and bans the latter.

3. There are situations when Christianity does condemn wine.

Let us take the first point:

1. Christianity does not ban the substance:

The substance in itself is not forbidden, otherwise God

would not have created it. But to what extent should we apply this rule to wine?

The most dangerous thing about wine is its alcoholic content, and Christianity does not ban alcohol as a substance.

Alcohol is used in medicine, in cleaning materials, in perfumes, and is put into the constituents of many medicines, besides having other beneficial uses. Therefore it is not prohibited in itself, and we cannot ban it. But when alcohol is abused it is prohibited.

The ban is on the misuse of the substance and not on the substance itself.

Let us take drugs as an example:

We forbid their abuse, because drugs ruin a person's life, health and dignity, and wastes his money, and drives him to commit crime. Drugs, as substances, though, are not banned in themselves, for they are needed to anaesthetise during surgical operations; but this is to use the properties of drugs for a good purpose, in a healthy way, and one that doesn't lead to addiction. In fact, used in this way, the drug enters the subconscious, far away from the will, or desire, or yearnings of the patient whom the doctor is anaesthetising.

Even poisons are not 'bad' in themselves as some are used medicinally as part of treatment.

According to one of our poets:

"One poison can be antidote for another,
and what might otherwise poison, may well cure the incurable."

From this starting point, and according to this reasoning, we can go on to talk about wine: we do not prohibit wine in itself as a substance, but only its abuse, as I have said above, I shall now go on to explain exactly what this abuse is.

Wine was used in the past in treating illness before the science of pharmacy developed.

We notice this in the story of the Good Samaritan *(Luke 10:34)*, and in the advice given by Paul to his disciple Timothy, when he said: " *No longer drink only water, but use a little wine for your stomach's sake and your frequent infirmities.(1 Tim. 5:23)*.

And some elderly people whose bodies had lost a lot of their natural warmth, used to be given a little wine - as part of a cure - to help restore the warmth that their bodies required.

In a similar way, people in certain countries which are bitterly cold, take some wine to keep themselves warm, which is the opposite to our hot country, where many people's bodies are badly affected by the excessive heat.

2. Wine and intoxicants:

The Holy Bible draws a clear distinction between wine and intoxicating spirits.

Among the many verses which show this, I could mention:

1. *"Do not drink wine or intoxicating drink, you, nor your sons with you, when you go into the tabernacle of meeting, lest you die." (Lev. 10:9)*

2. And he said to the mother of that giant, Samson, when she was carrying him: *" Now therefore, please be careful not to drink wine or similar drink, and not to eat anything unclean." (Judg. 13:4).* And he also said to her husband, Samson's father: *"Your wife... may not eat anything that comes from the vine, nor may she drink wine or similar drink, nor eat anything unclean. All that I commanded her let her observe."(Judg. 13:14).*

3. **And it was said of John the Baptist:** *"He shall drink neither wine nor strong drink.. " (Luke 1:15).*

Thus in each case there was a clear distinction between wine and stronger forms of drink.

But what is the basic difference between them? And how can we distinguish between them?

The essential difference is the amount of alcohol that each contains, and by this we can distinguish between two types

of wine: that produced by fermentation, and that produced by distillation.

Wine that is produced by natural fermentation may contain no more than 5 or 6% alcohol, and this is what we use in Church during the Eucharist, and it comes under the heading of 'wine'. We mean by this the kind of wine which is not intoxicating, and the person only takes a very few drops from it, a part of a small spoonful mixed with water during the service.

Liquor or spirits prepared by distillation, however, may contain sometimes as much as 50% alcohol, or thereabouts. It is 'this which comes under the heading of 'intoxicating drinks', and we prohibit them because the Bible does so, as I have shown above.

3. The Abuse of Wine:

This is something forbidden, and here are some cases and examples of such wrong use:
a) If it is harmful to a person's health and strength of mind and personality.

b) If it leads to drunkenness, or loss of physical control, to bad behaviour, or into areas of immorality.

c) If it is addictive, making a person drink more and more until it becomes a habit difficult to break, or an addiction, which dominates him, so that he reaches a stage where he drinks for no reason and without needing to.

d) If it leads to harmful social consequences and frequently it does.

e) When it constitutes a stumbling block to others. *(Rom. 14:12)*

f) If one uses it on holy occasions, or in holy places (apart from in the Eucharist of course) and then comes to serve God, having drunk alcohol. The Holy Bible forbids drinking wine for all the reasons mentioned above. There are world-wide Christian associations for the prohibition of intoxicants.

One of the reasons for banning these intoxicants is because of the harm which they can do to a person's health.

The Bible says: *"Do not not mix with winebibbers.. for drunkards.. become poor. " (Prov. 23:20)*

And regarding their prohibition on account of their power to cause drunkenness and physical instability and lead to depravity.

The apostle Paul says: *"Do not be drunk with wine, in which is dissipation. " (Eph. 5:18).* Here Paul mentions two harmful consequences of drinking alcohol: drunkenness and debauchery. The Bible also says: *"Wine is a mocker, Strong drink is a brawler, And whoever is led astray by it is not wise." (Prov. 20:1)*

A distinction is made here between wine and beer. The phrase 'whoever is led astray by them', however, means someone who drinks too much to remain sober, for even though the degree of alcohol in the particular wine or alcoholic drink might not be very great, it obviously mounts up when a large quantity is consumed, which would then lead to drunkenness. The Bible condemns anyone who makes his friend drunk with too much alcohol. *(Hab. 2:15)*

The Bible forbids drunkards from entering the kingdom of heaven *(1 Cor. 6:10)*, and forbids any association with drunkards *(1 Cor. 5:11)*

When it comes to banning wine for its harmful effects, the Bible says: "*Who has woe? Who has sorrow? Who has contentions? Who has complaints? Who has wounds without cause? Who has redness of eyes? Those who linger long at the wine, Those who go in search of mixed wine." (Prov. 23:29-30)*

Here we see how the Bible heaps doom and destruction on those who are addicted to wine.

The Bible says also: "*Do not look on the wine when it is red, When it sparkles in the cup, When it swirls around smoothly; At the last it bites like a serpent, And stings like a viper.*" *(Prov. 23:31-32)* And about the harm caused by wine it says: "*Wine [is] a mocker, Strong drink [is] a brawler*" *(Prov. 20:1)*

There are many other verses concerning the prevention of addiction and over-indulgence, such as what Peter says about those who follow the road to evil:

"You have spent enough time in the past.. living in debauchery, lust, drunkenness..." (1 Pet. 4:3) (See also 1 Tim. 3:8, Titus 1:7 and 2:3).

And concerning the banning of wine on holy occasions:

The Lord said to Aaron: " *Do not drink wine or intoxicating drink, you, nor your sons with you, when you go into the tabernacle of meeting, lest you die.* " *(Lev. 10:9)* The Bible also says: *"No priest is to drink wine when he enters the inner court." (Ezek. 44:22)*

The prophet Daniel speaking about his period of fasting said: " *I ate no pleasant food, no meat or wine came into my mouth* " *(Dan. 10:3)*. And it says that when Daniel was in Nebuchadnezzar's Palace he: " *would not defile himself with the portion of the king's delicacies* " *(Dan. 1:8)*

It was forbidden for a Nazirite to drink wine. In fact he wasn't even allowed to drink grape juice. *(Num. 6:3)*

Kings also were not allowed to drink wine.

The Bible says regarding this:

" It is not for kings, O Lemuel, It is not for kings to drink wine, Nor for princes intoxicating drink;" (Prov. 31:4).

[35]

GOD'S WILL AND PERMISSION

Question?

If everything comes about according to the will of God, and nothing on the face of the earth happens without His command alone, then why doesn't He prevent evil before it happens?

Answer:

Before coming to the reply, let us make note of various errors in your question.

It is not correct to say that nothing happens on earth except by God's will, for various wrongs, evils, crimes and injustices take place all too frequently in the world, and how could all these be 'according to the will of God'? That would not be right at all. Could all the killing, the adultery,'-the theft, fraud and lying that goes on in the world, ever be in accordance with God's will?! No, of course not. And does God like all these things to happen?! No, not at all.

Therefore your words 'everything comes about according to the will of God', are theologically incorrect, because everything would have to include the bad as well as the good. When bad things take place, it can never be in

accordance with God's will, for God never desires what is bad.

God only ever wants what is good. He wants all to be saved, and all to accept the knowledge of the Truth. All the good that happens on earth to people, or by them comes about in accordance with the will of God, but not the evil. So what, then, is the position of evil in relation to God's will?

It was God who gave mankind free will. It is God who permits human beings to do as they wish, whether good or bad, otherwise they would be nothing but robots.

The good that man does, he does in accordance with God's will, while the bad things that he does, is tolerated by God, but does not meet with His approval. There is a difference between what God wills and what God permits. His will is only ever for what is good. But He tolerates what is not good, because it is the inevitable consequence of that freedom of choice which He has given to some of His creatures.

[36]

THE FRUITS OF SIN

Question?

I caused some people to stumble, and they fell badly into sin because of me. I then repented, but they have not yet done so. I still see the fruits of my original fall in the lives of those other people. Is my repentance sufficient for me to be forgiven?.

Answer:

This is a difficult question, and one that can have a far-reaching effect. Essentially it is this:

A person who repented, but those who have sinned because of him did not repent, does that person still bear the responsibility of their sin?

This question shows us how far and how deeply, and to what extent, sin can personally affect someone. A person may have abandoned his sin, but it can still have an effect on others, an effect which that person can see before him at all times. He will be saddened and will suffer as a result of this, and feel the extent of his responsibility for it. So what can he do?

He could conceivably do his utmost to try and get those others, whom he caused to fall, to repent. But what if they do not?

He can act for himself, but what can he do about the others? Obviously such a person will live a sad and painful life for a long time. Any joy that his repentance might have brought him, would not be able to make up for the pain that he feels on seeing the ruinous effects of his sin on others, especially if they have really turned out for the bad, or perished.

It is possible that the words, 'life for life.' loom before him, so that he cries out to God, saying: *"Deliver me from the guilt of bloodshed, O God, The God of my salvation " (Ps. 51:14).*

He may try to do whatever he can on behalf of the others, though he may not be able to do anything. Furthermore, his resuming contact with the others, may well be dangerous to him, and it may be best for him to keep well away from them lest he should be ruined as well.

Perhaps those whom he has caused to fall have themselves caused many others to fall too, so that the circle has widened. Besides the direct results of the sin, there are also indirect results. Is it not true that we cannot calculate the extent of our sins, and the degree of their influence?

The first piece of advice I would give the questioner is to be really and truly contrite, and humble himself before God,

praying for the souls of the others, that God may send them help to be saved.

Let him also set for himself days of fasting demanding from the Church prayers in the Holy Mass and making prostrations, on their behalf. And let him cry copious tears for their sakes, and remind himself of what the Lord said: " Woe to the world because of offenses! For offenses must come, but woe to that man by whom the offense comes!" (Matt. 18:7) Let him ask for repentance for all those people, and let him act on their behalf, even if it is somehow indirectly, and send them guides or Father Confessors.

And he who has repented will not perish because of them. Our example of this is St. Mary the Copt.

In the early part of her life, before she repented, she caused many thousands to stumble, and some may have perished because of her. But with her sincere and true repentance, she became a great saint, and she was forgiven for her past sins.

We must not forget, either, that those who fall into sin have willingly and knowingly entered into it, and consequently the full responsibility for their fall does not entirely rest on the person who caused them to stumble.

In fact they responded to the stumbling block and accepted it. Nevertheless, the one who urged them into sin, could say to himself: They are really weak, and have fallen, but it was I who provided the inducement for their weakness, and I didn't show consideration or pity for their lack of willpower. I should have protected them, and strengthened them, and not been the reason for them to fall. if it hadn't been for me, they might never have fallen.

This person is like a car driver who has run somebody over, and has caused that person to be permanently disabled, who, even though he has said that he is sorry for what he has done, and God has forgiven him, whenever he sees or thinks about the one whom he has crippled, feels very unhappy.

This sadness, however, would obviously help make his repentance even more acceptable.

[37]

THE SPIRITUAL LIFE AND TROUBLES

Question?

The nearer I get to God, the more trials, problems and difficulties I seem to have, so that I get fed up and weary with life. I can't seem to find a way out of this except by keeping away from God, so that I get a more comfortable and peaceful life, like all the other people who keep at a distance from God! Why does God let this happen to me?

Answer:

Whenever you follow the road to God, and grow in your spiritual life, the devils become jealous of you, and try to make you go far away from his path, which they do, for example, by causing the kind of troubles that are happening to you.

So if you keep away from God, and abandon the spiritual road, you will have fulfilled Satan's wish, and he will have overcome you in the battle.

Listen to the words of St. Paul: " *Do not be overcome by evil, but overcome evil with good* **"** *(Rom. 12:21).*

So when troubles start, be patient, and try to do even more good things, for then Satan will despair of you, and will see that the troubles he has given you have had the opposite effect, and so he will leave you to look for something else.

Trust that God's grace will stand beside you, will support you, and give you the victory. This way Satan will despair of you, instead of you despairing of God's mercies.
God's patience and lack of intervention to save you, at the beginning of your troubles, has simply been to test your heart and see how committed it is to God!.

And, do not imagine that those who live far away from God live in comfort.

Their consciences within bother them, and they have no peace of mind. And in the afterlife, they will live in constant turmoil, while on earth their sin also causes many troubles for them. If they do seem to have peace and comfort, it is not true peace or comfort.

Trust that any exertion made for the Lord will be rewarded, both on earth and in heaven, since " *each one will receive his own reward according to his own labor* " *(1 Cor. 3:8).*

The story of the rich man and poor Lazarus, gives us a clear picture of this subject. And the Lord Jesus Christ told us: " *In the world you will have tribulation* " *(John 16:33),* but He also assured us that even the hairs on our heads have been counted.

He promised us many consolations and comforts, and that He would lead us in His procession of victory.

So make sure that you understand well that your troubles do not come from God, but from Satan who is envious of you. Our father the apostle James said: " Let no one say when he is tempted, "*I am tempted by God*"; " *(James 1:13)*

So, do you want to abandon God, who has never caused you any trouble, and join forces with Satan, who does cause you troubles? Do you want to be like someone who becomes an enemy to his friends, and befriends his enemies?!

Be patient, then, and receive the blessing and the crown for having endured troubles, and have faith that God will give you rest, because He said: " *Come to Me, all you who labor and are heavy laden, and I will give you rest.* " *(Matt. 11:28)*. And say to yourself: What are my troubles compared to those endured by the saints and martyrs on the Lord's behalf?!

[38]

BEING PERFECT
WHAT DOES IT MEAN ? AND
WHAT ARE ITS LIMITS

Question?

The Bible says: " *Therefore you shall be perfect, just as your Father in heaven is perfect* **" (Matt. 5:48) What does it mean to be 'perfect', and how can a human being attain it? When can we say of a person that he is 'perfect'?.**

Answer:

Absolute perfection belongs to God alone, no human being can ever attain it, because we will all be found wanting, when weighed in the balance.

So the perfection which a human being can attain is a relative perfection.

The state of perfection he can reach will be in relation to his abilities, his possibilities, and the extent of heavenly grace bestowed upon him.

The Lord God, speaking of the righteous Job said: " *that man was blameless and upright, and one who feared God and* shunned evil." and " there is none like him on the earth " *(Job 1:1 & 8)*. Job's 'perfection', was only relative not absolute perfection.

In the same sense, Noah was said to have been a righteous and God-fearing man: " *Noah was a just man, perfect in his generations. Noah walked with God. " (Gen. 6:9)*.

Jacob too was perfect, even though he had various weaknesses. *(Gen. 25:27)*. But God judges each human being in relation to each one's possibilities, according to the era in which he lives, his level and the work of the Spirit within him.

The quality of being perfect might be in relation to a particular commandment, such as when the Lord Jesus said to the rich young man: *"If you want to be perfect, go, sell your possessions and give to the poor. " (Matt. 19:21)*

It is our duty to strive for perfection, but we can never say that we have reached it. In any case, the road to perfection consists of stages, so that as soon as a person reaches one of them he finds another higher, further stage awaiting him, and he becomes like someone pursuing the horizon.

Look at St. Paul, the apostle who ascended to the third heaven, and who laboured harder than all the other apostles, who said:

"Not that I have already attained, or am already perfected; but I press on... But one thing I do, forgetting those things which are behind and reaching forward to those things which are ahead. " (Phil. 3:12-14)

If the great St Paul did not consider that he had become perfect, but that he needed to strive and strain to reach it, what can we say about ourselves?

Even so, Paul said directly after this: " *Therefore let us, as many as are mature, have this mind;* " *(Phil. 3:15),* where he is referring to all those who might have thought that they were 'perfect', or whom other people might have considered to have attained that stage.

A pupil in primary school may reach the highest grade in mathematics, and they might say that he has become perfect, at that level. But as he gets older, he then moves up from the level of 'perfection' in the primary school, to the level of ‚perfection' in his junior school, and then to the highest level in his high school, and so on until university. But each standard of 'perfection' is relative, and even so, he would never consider himself to have become 'perfect' in mathematics for there are always higher and higher levels to reach.

[39]

PEOPLE WHO HAVE CONFESSED BUT WHOSE SINS HAVE NOT BEEN FORGIVEN

Question?

What is your view on people who have confessed, but whose sins have not been forgiven, like Pharaoh, who confessed his sin to Moses *(Ex. 9:27)*, and Achan son of Carmi, who confessed to Joshua *(Josh. 7:20)*, and King Saul who confessed to Samuel the prophet *(1 Sam. 15:24-26)?*.

Answer:

The sacrament of confession in the Church is also called the sacrament of repentance. A person must show himself repentant before coming to confess his sins. Confession without being sorry for your sins is of no value. And one who confesses cannot obtain forgiveness unless he is repentant.

Those whom you mentioned confessed, but were not repentant. Pharaoh cried out: "I have sinned", but his heart was still hard within. He was not motivated by remorse, but by fear of the plagues, for as soon as each plague was lifted, he revealed himself in his true nature.

Achan the Son of Carmi didn't go to Joshua confessing and repentant, but God revealed his sin against his will, so he was forced to admit his fault. The whole nation was defeated, but Achan did not confess. The Lord said: *"Israel has sinned.. they have even taken some of the accursed things, and have both stolen and deceived " (Josh. 7:11),* yet Achan did not own up. Then began the casting of lots and the threats, but still he would not admit it. Even when the finger was pointed on his own tribe and on his own clan and on his own household, Achan did not confess. So in the end the Lord exposed him by name, and he was forced to own up. Was he then, in spite of all this, repentant?

King Saul was not repentant, even when he said: "I have sinned". His only object was to get Samuel to go back with him. He did not act out of regret at what he had done, but for the sake of keeping his honour, so that he could lift up his face before the people!! This is why he said: *" yet honor me now, please, before the elders of my people and before Israel. " (1 Sam. 15:30).*

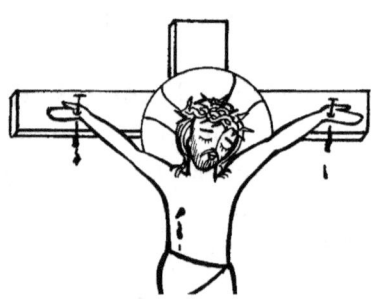

[40]

THE SPIRITUALITY OF THE MONKS AND LAYMEN

Question?

Does God require more in terms of prayers, fasting, devotion, etc., from the father monks than from laypeople?.

Answer:

Yes, undoubtedly. More is required of the monks because they are in a situation of complete dedication to the Lord, in contrast to laypeople who have other commitments which distract them. Even so, all are required to strive for holiness and perfection.

The Lord Jesus said: " *be perfect, just as your Father in heaven is perfect." (Matt. 5:48)* This commandment was intended for all people, long before the monastic orders arose.

The degrees of perfection and holiness which each person can attain, however, differ from one individual to another.

When it comes to prayers, the seven prayers are required of every Orthodox believer, and David the prophet, even though he had many responsibilities as king, used to pray them, as he says in his psalm: " *Seven times a day I praise You, Because of Your righteous judgments." (Ps. 119:164)* Likewise the night prayers are required of all, and David prayed them too. *(Ps. 119:148).*

The rituals of the monks, though, involve constant, uninterrupted prayers.

This is something which laypeople cannot do because of their need to spend time in work and with their families and in various activities and services. Nevertheless, the commandment is to, *"pray without ceasing," (1 Thes. 5:17),* and, *"men always ought to pray and not lose heart. " (Luke 18:1),* and this was addressed to all people, long before monasticism.

Every individual ought to persevere in prayer as much as they can.

When it comes to fasting, all Orthodox believers, except for babies, children, pregnant and nursing women, old people and those who are unwell, are all required to observe all the fasts of the Coptic Church.

The monks, on the other hand, have their own special ritual which involves certain degrees of abstinence. Some of them might abstain wholly from food for days and do not eat any tasty kinds of food. And there are monasteries where no flesh foods are eaten at all.

The asceticism of the monks also with regard to their garments again differs from that of laypeople who live in a society with all its particular demands.

[41]

JESUS CHRIST AND THE COMPLETION OF HIS MISSION

Question?

Is it correct that the Lord Jesus Christ did not complete His mission, but will complete it on the day of His rising up to life?.

Answer:

The work of Christ, as far as His divinity is concerned, is everlasting, eternal, and to this apply the words: " *My Father has been working until now, and I have been working.* " *(John 5:17)*.

As for the time of His incarnation the Lord Jesus completed the work for which He had come, which was to redeem the world and to save us all from the penalty of sin, for: *"the Son of Man came to seek and to save what was lost.* " *(John 19:30)*. Concerning this mission He said on the cross: *"It is finished"* *(John 19:30)*

Christ's work as a mediator on our behalf, however, is something constant for all time, as the apostle said *(1 John 2:1)*.

There is another kind of work which Christ will perform at the end of time, when He comes in His second coming, which is, to judge the living and the dead, and to give to each person according to his deeds. *(Matt. 24:25; Rev. 22)*.

Even in eternity His work will not stop...

We can never say about any period of time that 'Christ's mission has not been completed', that would be an inaccurate statement, and would suggest that He had failed in some way. But we can say that he had many missions: the first was in the very beginning, " *through Him, and without Him nothing was made that was made." (John 1:3),* followed by various kinds of work, each one of which was completed fully, such as His work during the period of His incarnation on earth before the crucifixion, in teaching, guiding, making disciples, spreading the faith, and preparing the way for the concept of the cross to be accepted. It was about this that He said to the Father: *"I have glorified You on the earth. I have finished the work which You have given Me to do " (John 17:4)*

After His ascension into heaven, there was another kind of work which He did, which was to send the Holy Spirit. And this happened on the day of Pentecost. *(Acts 2)*

As for your words, 'when He rises up to life'. the answer to this is that the Lord Jesus Christ has already risen. He rose on the third day after His crucifixion, and all the apostles witnessed it. Besides, in His divine nature the Lord has always been alive and will never die.

[42]

THOUGHTS OF SELF-RIGHTEOUSNESS

Question?

What should I do when Satan attacks me with thoughts of self righteousness?.

Answer:

There are two basic methods of fighting thoughts of self-righteousness, and they are for a person to remember his sins, and to recall the highest stages reached by the saints.

Recalling his sins will make a person humble, contrite and ashamed, because even a single sin can cause him to perish. Likewise, bringing to mind the highest stages which the saints attained in each form of virtue, will make a person realise how insignificant he is if he should compare himself to that level.

We must also attribute to God's grace, any virtue or goodness that we might have done, and must remember that self-righteousness will make God's grace forsake us and leave us to fall.. which would soon make us aware of our weakness and return to a humble position.

So you have to remember to be afraid of falling, whenever you submit to thoughts of self-righteousness because, 'Pride goes before a fall'.

[43]

WHO AM I? AND WHY HAVE I COME HERE?

Question?

Who am I? Why have I come here? And why should I live and die?.

Answer:

This subject may be answered in a whole book, but I will try to answer you briefly.

1. Who am I?

*. You are a human being, created in the image and likeness of God *(Gen. 1:26),* and you must try and preserve this divine image.

*. You are a living being with a rational spirit, whose life does not end with death, but will continue. You have a conscience to distinguish between good and evil, and are enlightened by the Spirit of God dwelling within you. *(1 Cor. 3:16).*

*. You are distinct from other earthly creatures by having an intelligent mind, with all that it contains in the way of understanding and perception.

*. With your mind and will you are responsible for your deeds, firstly before God, secondly before your own conscience, and thirdly before the society in which you live.

*. Whether you receive a reward, or a punishment, in the afterlife, after the judgement before God, will depend on how responsible you have been during your lifetime.

2. Why have I come here?

It is out of His goodness that God has given you the gift of being alive.

Out of His generosity and unselfishness He has given you the opportunity to be, to enjoy life here on earth, and to have a chance to live in eternal happiness, if you wish to, and if you act in such a way as to deserve it.

3. Why am I alive?

You are alive in order to carry out a mission, towards yourself and towards others, in order to enjoy and experience God, here on earth, and to, *"Taste and see that the Lord is good. " (Ps. 34:8).*
And also your willpower is put to the test during your lifetime, to see to what extent it is drawn to good or evil. Your life is a period of testing to see if you are deserving of the kingdom of heaven, and to define what degree of life you are to enjoy in eternity. You have to recognise and carry out your mission,

and be a blessing for the generation in which you live. The extent to which your mission is powerful and productive will determine the extent to which your life on earth and in heaven is exalted.

And why should I die?

You should die so that you will be able to pass on to a better life, which was refered to as: "*Eye has not seen, nor ear heard, Nor have entered into the heart of man...*" *(1 Cor. 2:9)*. You can then also move into the most wonderful companionship of all, that of God, His angels and His saints. Therefore death is not passing away to destruction, but passing on to another life.

If your life on earth were just to go on and on, you would remain attached to material things and united to the earthly body, which would not be good for you. It is better, though, for you to move on from the life of material things and the body, to the life of the spirit and of eternity, and to be with Christ, *"which is far better." (Phil. 1:23)*. This is why the saints so yearned to be released from this earthly body. Those who fear death are those who are not prepared for it, and who do not trust that they will pass on to a better life... or who have earthly desires which they don't want to give up!!

Man dies, because death is better for the world. It would be unconceivable if people were to live without ever dying, and if generation were to follow generation on and on, the earth would not have enough space, the elderly would be overburdened by the increasing weight of old age, and would need people to serve them, care for them and help shoulder their burdens. Thus each generation has to die in order to give the next generation the chance to live on earth and to take its rightful place in the scheme of things.

[44]

PRAYERS AND PROSTRATIONS

Question?

What prayers should be said when performing prostrations?

Answer:

They could be prayers of humbling oneself before God and confessing one's sins before Him, along with asking for mercy. For each prostration, the individual can confess a sin and accuse himself before God with the words: 'Have mercy on me, O God, for I have done such and such'.

They could be prayers of thanksgiving in which the person brings to mind God's mercies to him or to his loved ones, and in each prostration he can recall some of God's good gifts.

They could be prayers of petition, in which the one praying mentions something that he would like to have personally, or he wishes that God grants to the Church or to someone else. In fact prostrations can be accompanied by any such suitable kind of prayer.

CONTENTS

	Introduction
1.	The origin of bad thoughts
2.	Envy
3.	Should one give tithes to relatives?
4.	My own financial needs and paying the tithes
5.	Being nosey about prying into other people's business
6.	Is this vow permissible or forbidden?
7.	The first sin
8.	Responsibility for a sin which one has not committed
9.	Is social service the work of the Church or that of the State?
10.	Hymns sung to popular tunes
11.	How to resist thoughts
12.	Loving one's enemies
13.	Punishment and the age of grace.
14.	What does "to the Jews I became like a Jew" mean?.
15.	How to deal with problems
16.	Acting quickly or taking one's time
17.	In private or in public
18.	Criticism and condemnation
19.	Should the sacraments be sold
20.	What does "I have kept you from sinning against Me" mean?

21. Sins are not equal in degree, nor in punishment
22. The view of Christianity regarding organ transplants
23. How should we pray?
24. About asking for gifts
25. The highest virtue of all
26. Following the lives of the saints
27. Whether it is necessary to know how to read and write in order to enter a religious institution..
28. The meek will inherit the earth
29. Free time
30. Everyone who has will be given more
31. The real elements of strength
32. If your eye or hand causes you to sin
33. Simplicity
34. The attitude of Christianity towards wine.
35. God's will and permission
36. The fruits of sin
37. The spiritual life and problems
38. Being perfect - what it means and what its limits are
39. People who have confessed but whose sins have not been forgiven
40. The spirituality of the monks and laymen 151.
41. Jesus Christ and the completion of His mission
42. Thoughts of self-righteousness
43. Who am I? And why have I come here?
44. Prayers and prostrations